Cupcakes

for Any Occasion

Cupcakes
for Any Occasion

Rachel Lindsay
@cakedbyrach

Publisher Mike Sanders
Art & Design Director William Thomas
Editorial Director Ann Barton
Senior Editor Brook Farling
Editorial Assistant Resham Anand
Designer Lissa Auciello
Photographer Harriet Harcourt
Copy Editor Jean Bissell
Proofreaders Mira S. Park, Lisa Starnes
Indexer Michael Goldstein

First American Edition, 2025
Published in the United States by DK Publishing
1745 Broadway, 20th Floor, New York, NY 10019

The authorized representative in the EEA is Dorling Kindersley
Verlag GmbH. Arnulfstr. 124, 80636 Munich, Germany

Copyright © 2025 Rachel Lindsay
DK, a Division of Penguin Random House LLC
25 26 27 28 29   10 9 8 7 6 5 4 3 2 1
001-344013-MAR2025

A catalog record for this book
is available from the Library of Congress.
ISBN 978-0-5939-5804-9

DK books are available at special discounts when purchased
in bulk for sales promotions, premiums, fund-raising, or
educational use. For details, contact SpecialSales@dk.com

Printed and bound in Slovakia

www.dk.com

MIX
Paper | Supporting
responsible forestry
FSC™ C018179

This book was made with Forest
Stewardship Council™ certified
paper – one small step in DK's
commitment to a sustainable future.
Learn more at
www.dk.com/uk/information/sustainability

To Conor, Liam, and Ronan

Introduction

Hi, and welcome to my book. I'm so glad you are here, and if I'm being totally honest, I can't believe that *we* are here. Creating book has been a massive dream of mine ever since I started my cake decorating journey. I'm still pinching myself to see if this is real—a book of my very own to share with you.

I feel so lucky every day that I get to do something I love and that I get to share it with my followers on my social media platforms. Whether you are a hobby baker or a professional, my aim for this book is to inspire you with my bright and bold designs. I love to make cupcakes that are full of fun and are a little on the extra side. All of these projects are guaranteed to bring the WOW factor to any occasion.

I often get asked how I come up with my ideas, and my response is that inspiration is all around us and the possibilities are endless. I believe that creativity breeds creativity, so the more you practice the more your ideas will flow and your own personal style will develop. There is room to adapt any of these designs and make them your own. The most important thing to remember is to have fun. The love and effort that you put into a creation is what will make it special. Cupcakes are made to be eaten, so just enjoy the process.

I think that there can be and should be a cupcake for any occasion, and in this book I have created 50 projects for you to pick and choose from. No matter what the occasion, there is a design for you.

The chapters are divided into techniques, recipes, and projects. I have included my favorite cupcake and buttercream recipes that I have never shared before. You can mix and match the flavors to suit your tastes and the occasion. And if you don't feel like baking, you can use the decorating projects to jazz up store-bought cupcakes or even use a cake mix if you prefer; there is no judgment here, though I do recommend using my homemade buttercream recipes for the best results. The store-bought stuff just won't work the same.

I share my best tips and techniques with photos to show you how I achieve some of my unique designs. I walk you through each project with step-by-step tutorials, and if needed you can refer to the techniques section as you work through the projects. After making a few of the projects, you won't believe how easy it can be!

I hope you get as much enjoyment out of this book as I have had creating it for you.

Practice makes perfect, whatever perfect is to you.

Happy cupcaking!

Rachel xx

Contents

Introduction 6

chapter 1
The Basics 11

Essential Equipment 12

Basic Ingredients 14

Working with Piping Bags 15

Coloring Buttercream 17

Using the Flip-and-Freeze
Method 18

Piping a Multicolored Swirl 19

Creating Shaped Cupcakes 20

Working with Candy Melts 21

chapter 2
Buttercream &
Cupcake Recipes 23

Vanilla and Flavored Cupcakes 24

Chocolate Cupcakes 25

Red Velvet Cupcakes 26

Peanut Butter and Jelly Cupcakes 27

Carrot Cupcakes 28

Lemon Cupcakes 29

Rainbow Cupcakes 30

Chai Latte Cupcakes 31

Cookie Dough Cupcakes 32

Basic Buttercream 33

Chocolate Buttercream 34

Oreo Buttercream 34

Swiss Meringue Buttercream 35

Cream Cheese Buttercream 36

Hybrid Buttercream 36

Black Buttercream 37

chapter 3
Holidays 39

Love Hearts 40

Love Monsters 43

Shamrocks 47

Pots of Gold 51

Bunny Butts 54

Easter Chicks 56

Bird Nests 59

Easter Baskets 63

Mister Brain 66

Spooky Skulls 69

Witches' Hats 73

Ghosts 77

Turkeys 81

Oh My, Pumpkin Pies! 85

Shaped Christmas Trees 89

Snow-Covered Christmas Trees 93

Frosty and Friends (Snowmen) 97

Santas 101

chapter 4

Special Occasions 105

Wedding Day 107

Happy Birthday! 111

Birthday Magic! 115

High Heels (Bridal Showers) 119

Graduation Caps 122

It's a Baby! (Baby Showers or
Gender Reveals) 125

Mother's Day Flower Power
(Daisies and Sunflowers) 131

chapter 5

Seasonal 135

Campfires 137

BBQ Grills 141

Toadstools 145

Butterflies 149

Beach Vibes 153

Flower Pots 157

Cactuses 161

Pine Cones 165

Pumpkin Patch 169

chapter 6

Food 173

Melting Ice Creams 175

Hot Dogs 178

Cheeseburgers 181

Spaghetti and Meatballs 184

Fruit Pies 187

Sushi Train 191

Happy Avocados 195

Pineapples 199

chapter 7

Animals 203

Turtle-y Awesome 205

Kings of the Jungle (Lions) 209

Sleepy Sloths 213

Bunnies 217

Hip Hop Hooray! (Frogs) 221

Pigs in the Mud 225

Penguins 228

Pupcakes 231

Acknowledgments 234

Index 236

About the Author 240

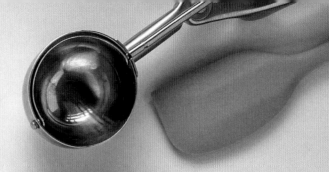

chapter 1

The Basics

Essential Equipment. 12

Basic Ingredients. 14

Working with Piping Bags 15

Coloring Buttercream 17

Using the Flip-and-Freeze
   Method 18

Piping a Multicolored Swirl 19

Creating Shaped Cupcakes. 20

Working with Candy Melts. 21

Essential Equipment

You don't need to have a fully equipped kitchen to use this book. And if you like to bake, chances are you probably have lots of these items already. This is a list of things that I use every day and couldn't do without when I'm baking and creating.

Baking trays: I use my baking trays all the time, but less so for baking and more so for transferring things to and from the fridge or freezer. Having one that will fit in the fridge or freezer is a must.

Cupcake liners: I love to use foil cupcake liners when I'm baking; I think they look nicer, and they don't end up with a greasy bottom. They come in a variety of colors, too. You can use regular liners for most projects, but when you are making shaped cupcakes, foil liners work best because they can be pinched and shaped to help form the cupcake shape.

Cupcake pans: I have several 12-cup cupcake pans, but I do make lots of cupcakes. You really only need one or two for home baking. The pan I use is a 10.5 × 15-inch (26.5 × 38cm) Wilton with a cavity size of 2 inches (d) × 1.25 inches (5cm [d] × 3.25cm). Be sure to get a cupcake pan and not a muffin tin, as they are larger. A 24-cup mini cupcake pan is also great to have.

Digital scale: I can't stress enough how important weighing scales are when it comes to baking. Baking is a science, which is why recipes have exact measurements. I don't use cup measurements. And I even weigh my liquids.

Kitchen timer: I always use a digital kitchen timer when baking and mixing ingredients. It's so easy to lose track of time and burn a perfect batch of cupcakes, so having a simple digital kitchen timer on hand will be a lifesaver.

Knives: Be sure to have a sharp, high-quality knife and a small serrated knife. I use these for decorating as well.

Large cookie dough scoop: I use a cookie dough scoop to fill my cupcake liners with batter. A large scoop will hold about 3 tablespoons of batter, and it's a great way to ensure uniformly sized cupcakes.

Measuring spoons: Although I'm not a fan of measuring cups, I do use measuring spoons for small-volume measurements. Spoon measurements are level unless the recipe states a "heaped" spoon; otherwise, you should always level off your measuring spoon with the ingredient you are measuring.

Mixing bowls: Mixing bowls of all different sizes always get used a lot in my kitchen. I have several large and medium ones, and I have lots of small ones for mixing colors into buttercreams.

Oven thermometer: All ovens are different, and their internal temperatures can be, too. (I learned this the hard way.) Knowing the actual temperature of your oven, not just the temperature you set it to, can make a world of difference when it comes to baking.

Palette knives: A small offset palette knife can be used to apply buttercream to your cupcakes and help you achieve a smooth buttercream finish. You can usually find an inexpensive set of palette knives through online resources like Amazon.com.

Parchment paper, cling film, and aluminum foil: I use these items a lot, and I always have a spare roll of each in the cupboard. There's nothing worse than running out of these in the middle of a project.

Piping bags: Piping bags come in different sizes—my most used sizes are 12-inch (30cm) and 18-inch

(45cm). The thick plastic bags are the sturdiest—Wilton or Ateco brands are both good—and can be bought in bulk on Amazon.com. You can also buy clips to secure the bags from the same sources, or you can just use rubber bands to secure the tops of the piping bags.

Rubber spatulas: Rubber spatulas are my favorite utensils in the kitchen. You can never have enough of these, and they come in all different sizes. They're amazing tools for scraping, scooping, and stirring.

Stand mixer: Most recipes in this book call for a stand mixer. I use a KitchenAid stand mixer, which I would be lost without; it saves so much time and effort. When I first started baking, I used an inexpensive handheld electric mixer; it got the job done and will work fine if that's what you have. I eventually worked up to a stand mixer.

Toothpicks: Having a pot of toothpicks on hand is essential. I use them for coloring buttercream, decorating, and checking if my cupcakes are baked.

Tweezers: I use these frequently when I'm decorating cupcakes and have several sets. I like the long tweezers with the pointed ends best. They work amazingly well for attaching sprinkles and small nonpareils to buttercream, which helps prevent finger holes and unwanted marks in your creations.

Whisk: I use a whisk with the metal loop; it's stronger than a plastic whisk and works better.

A Guide to Piping Tips

There are so many different types of piping tips available and owning them all is just not necessary. (I have a lot that I don't know what to do with, and some that I just never use.)

You can buy plastic or metal piping tips, but I always use and recommend metal tips. I think they give a sharper finish than the plastic tips, and they will last for years if you look after them.

Piping tips are assigned different numbers based on the shapes and sizes of their openings. The numbers given to them are universal across brands. A lot of cheaper, generic tips that you will find online won't have numbers on them; therefore, I recommend sticking with the tips with numbers that are listed in this book. The ones I use are mostly from Wilton, but I also have some of the jumbo tips from Ateco. You can purchase them individually from cake decorating stores, craft stores (like Michaels), retail stores (like Walmart), directly from suppliers, or online sites.

Here's a list of the tips used in this book:

- Round piping tips: 1A, 2A, 3, 4, 7, 10, 12
- Open star piping tips: 18, 21, 32, 4B, 8B, 1M
- Leaf piping tips: 70, 352, 366
- Grass piping tip: 233
- Basketweave piping tips: 46, 48, 2B
- Ateco jumbo piping tip: 809

You can buy piping tips in sets, or you can buy them individually. The sets are great when you are just starting out. Though you soon can start to double up on tips and be left with a lot that you will never use. You can purchase sets online or from cake supply shops.

Basic Ingredients

Most ingredients used for baking and decorating can be found at a regular supermarket. The more specialized items used for decorating can be easily found at cake supply shops, cake supply websites, or through online sites like Amazon.com.

Black cocoa powder: Black cocoa powder is basically cocoa powder that has been heavily Dutched or alkalized. The easiest way to describe the taste is to relate it to an Oreo cookie. The dark color of the cocoa helps create a dark base for black buttercream, meaning you won't need to add much food gel to achieve a rich black color. This can be bought from online sources, as it's not easy to find in normal shops.

Candy melts: Candy melts are an easy-to-use alternative to chocolate, with no tempering required. They come in a variety of colors and flavors. The brand I use is Wilton, though there are many different brands available. You can purchase these from cake decorating supply shops or online.

Caster sugar: Caster sugar is a white sugar with a fine grain, and because of this, it dissolves more easily than granulated sugar. It is also called *superfine sugar*.

Cocoa powder: To ensure that chocolate flavor is as chocolatey as it can be, I recommend using a good-quality cocoa powder in your bakes. Hershey's or Ghirardelli unsweetened cocoas are good and can be found in most supermarkets.

Confectioners' sugar: Also known as powdered sugar or icing sugar, I always sift confectioners' sugar into the ingredients when I'm making buttercreams to ensure there are no lumps.

Desiccated coconut: Desiccated coconut is a dried coconut product made by grating and dehydrating fresh coconut meat. It is much finer and drier than shredded coconut and has a powdery consistency.

Eggs: I use large free-range eggs for all of my recipes. I always let the eggs come to room temperature before using them; this helps them mix better with the batter and rise more easily, creating a fluffier cupcake.

Flavorings: There are many different choices when it comes to adding flavors to your cupcakes and buttercreams. You can buy a variety of flavors that come in oil form, which are highly concentrated and sold in specialized cake supply shops. Or, you can buy flavored extracts like orange, lemon, almond, and peppermint from the supermarket. You can also use natural ingredients to add amazing flavors.

Flour: I mostly use self-rising flour in my recipes. This is all-purpose flour with a rising agent added to it. You can make your own self-rising flour by adding 2 teaspoons of baking powder to 150g of all-purpose flour. However, this homemade version can add a slightly bitter taste to your bakes.

Fondant: Fondant can be store-bought or homemade. I only use small amounts, so I find it easier to use the brands that can be bought in a selection of colors from a cake supplier or a supermarket.

Food coloring: There are lots of choices when it comes to food colorings. Avoid using the liquids that you buy in the supermarkets: they are not concentrated enough and will ruin your recipes. I only use gel colors from Wilton or AmeriColor; they have a huge range of colors and will work great for coloring your cupcakes and buttercreams. I also use oil-based colors from Colour Mill. These work well for adding color to chocolate and candy melts, as well as cupcakes and buttercreams. You can buy these online or find them in some retailers like Walmart or Michaels, at cake supply shops, or online.

Sanding sugar: Sanding sugar is a decorative sugar that is great for decorating. It has a large crystal structure that reflects the light to create a sparkly effect. It comes in a variety of colors and can be purchased in some supermarkets, at cake supplies stores, or online.

Sprinkles and decorations: Most quality decorations like sprinkles and edible glitter will need to be purchased from a cake decorating supply shop or online.

Unsalted butter: I always use unsalted butter in my baking; it enables me to control how much salt is added to the buttercream or cupcakes. For best results, the butter should be softened before using. To tell if butter is softened properly, press into the middle of the butter with your finger. It should leave an indent with little to no resistance.

Vanilla extract: For the best tasting results, use a good-quality vanilla extract or vanilla bean paste. Avoid using vanilla essence, as it is artificial.

Working with Piping Bags

Using a piping bag is a simple process, but there are a few simple steps you should follow to ensure success with your projects.

1. Open the piping bag and drop the tip inside. Measure with your finger how much you need to cut off at the end of the bag. It should be just enough that the opening of the piping tip isn't covered by the bag, but not so much that the tip could fall through it. *(see Photo 1 on next page)*

2. Push the tip up and out of the way slightly and then use a pair of scissors to cut off just enough of the end of the bag to secure the tip. Push the piping tip back down into the hole so the end is poking out of the bottom of the bag. *(see Photo 2 on next page)*

3. To fill the bag, place the bag into a tall glass and fold the top of the bag over the edges of the glass. Use a rubber spatula to push the buttercream down to the bottom of the bag and toward the tip. Only fill the bag half to three-quarters full, leaving space at the top to secure the bag and hold onto while decorating. (This will also make refilling the bag a lot easier.) Twist the top of the bag and then secure it with a rubber band or clip until ready to use. *(see Photo 3 on next page)*

4. To use the piping bag, hold the top of the piping bag with your dominant hand. Place your thumb and four fingers around the twisted part of the bag and squeeze. (You can use your other hand to guide the piping bag.) Keep the pressure steady when you are piping and release it when you want to stop. As the bag starts to empty, stop and twist the bag to push the remaining buttercream toward the tip. *(see Photo 4 on next page)*

To refill a nearly empty bag, remove the clip and pop the bag back into a tall glass. Fold the top of the bag over the edges, then add the buttercream to the bag as you did previously.

Reusing Piping Bags

I like to use the plastic disposable piping bags, so I wash them and reuse them as many times as I can. When you have finished piping the buttercream, squeeze as much of the buttercream as you can into a resealable container and then lay the bag flat. Use a spatula to push the remaining buttercream down toward the tip and then squeeze it out. Turn the piping bag inside out and wash it in hot, soapy water. Let the bags dry completely before reusing them.

Coloring Buttercream

There are many different brands of food coloring on the market, but the brands I use and recommend are Wilton and AmeriColor, or the Colour Mill brand of oil-based colors.

Types of Food Colors

Gel colors are water-based and highly concentrated, so you don't need much product to achieve a bright color. The water in these gels mixes well with products that contain a high water content. I recommend using gel colors with all of my buttercream recipes and for coloring cupcake batter.

Oil-based food colors are designed to blend with oils and fats to create bold and vibrant colors, so they are best used for recipes that use ingredients that contain high amounts of fats and oils, like chocolate, candy melts, and buttercreams. These colors work great with all my buttercream recipes, though the colors will develop and deepen over time. Because of this, try to color your buttercream a day ahead of decorating and allow it to sit overnight for super vibrant results.

How to Color Buttercream

The amount of color that needs to be added to a buttercream will vary depending on the shade that you want to achieve and the amount of buttercream you are coloring.

Begin by adding one drop of gel food coloring to the buttercream and mixing it in completely. Gradually add additional drops of the color until you reach the desired shade. (You can always add more color, but you can't take it out once you've mixed it in.) It's important to remember that the color will intensify over time, so for brighter colors, I recommend coloring your buttercream a day in advance of decorating. If you are aiming for a pale shade or are just adding color to a small amount of buttercream, use a toothpick to add the color gradually.

Using the Microwave Method to Deepen Color

This trick will deepen the color of your buttercream without the need to add too much color gel. Transfer one-quarter of the amount of buttercream you are coloring to a microwave-safe bowl, add a few drops of gel food coloring, and mix it well. Transfer the bowl to the microwave and heat for 8 seconds, then take the bowl out of the microwave and stir. You will see that the color has already deepened by a few shades. Continue microwaving the buttercream in short intervals, stirring each time, until the color has developed to the desired shade. Add the buttercream back to the rest of the batch and stir to combine.

Using the Flip-and-Freeze Method

This is a simple and effective technique to get the perfect flat-top effect when using buttercream. I like to think of this as creating a blank canvas on your cupcakes—the design possibilities are endless! When using this technique, I prefer to use my basic buttercream recipe.

1. Prepare a piping bag with buttercream and a large round piping tip. (I use the Ateco 809. It's easier to use large piping tips when your piping bag has a good amount of buttercream in it.) Hold the piping bag upright and directly above the center of the cupcake. Squeeze out the buttercream, slowly lifting the bag as you squeeze. When you have the desired amount (approximately 1½ inches [4cm] wide), release the pressure and pull the bag up and away. *(see Photo 1)*

2. Line a baking tray with parchment paper. (Choose a tray size that will fit into your freezer.) Hold the cupcake upside down and above the parchment paper, then gently push it straight down into the parchment. The buttercream will spread as you push. *(see Photo 2)*

3. Transfer the tray to the freezer for 15 to 20 minutes. The buttercream is set when it cleanly peels away from the parchment and has a smooth surface. If it leaves some of the buttercream, place the tray back in the freezer for a few more minutes. *(see Photo 3)*

4. Place the cupcakes upright on the tray, and keep them in the fridge until you are ready to decorate.

1

2

3

Piping a Multicolored Swirl

You can use this technique with as many colors as you like.

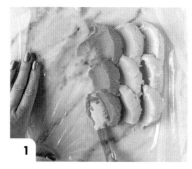

1. Make the individual buttercreams and color them.

2. Place a long piece of cling film on a flat surface. Use a rubber spatula to scoop the first colored buttercream onto the cling film, spreading it out in a long, horizontal line onto one end of the cling film. I recommend starting 2 inches (5cm) from the top edge of the cling film and keeping the line 2 inches (5cm) away from either side. Repeat with the remaining colors, lining them up next to each other. *(see Photo 1)*

3. Gently roll the cling film into a sausage shape. Lift one edge of the cling film and pull it over until the buttercream is cylindrical, then tuck in the edges and continue rolling it into a sausage shape. *(see Photo 2)*

4. Twist both ends of the cling film to secure the buttercream. *(see Photo 3)*

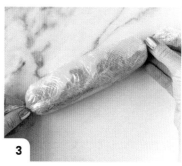

5. Fit the piping bag with the desired piping tip. Cut one end off of the buttercream sausage and add it to the piping bag. Twist the top of the bag and secure it with a rubber band or a clip until ready to use. *(see Photo 4)*

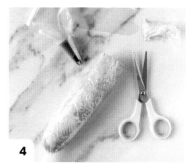

6. Pipe the multicolored buttercream into the desired shape. *(see Photo 5)*

The colors will start to blend slightly as they are being squeezed through the bag, which looks pretty. However, if you don't want the colors to blend and you want a striped result, wrap each color in an individual piece of cling film and then twist the ends to create a sausage shape. (The individual sausages should all be the same size.) Cut one end from each of the buttercream sausage shapes and align them next to each other in a piping bag that is already fitted with a piping tip.

Creating Shaped Cupcakes

Creating shaped cupcakes is a simple process, but there are a few important things to know as you create your shapes. The first is to use foil liners. You can pinch the edges of foil liners, which can help cupcakes hold their shapes during baking. The second is to use foil sheets that are cut to size. All of the projects in this book use 4 × 4-inch (10 × 10cm) sheets that are then either rolled into balls that can be placed outside the liners to help create shapes or are folded four times to create squares to create other shapes.

1. To create shaped cupcakes, fill a cupcake tray with foil liners and then fill the liners half full with batter. (Be careful not to overfill them, otherwise they can overflow and lose their shape during baking.) *(see Photo 1)*

2. Roll the foil sheets into different-size balls or fold them into smaller squares, depending on the cupcake shapes you are creating. Place the foil balls or squares on the outsides of the liners. *(see Photo 2)*

3. Pinch the edges of the liners around the foil balls or squares to hold them in place. *(see Photo 3)*

When you have the liners formed into the desired shapes, place the pan in the oven and bake the cupcakes according to the recipe instructions. Be sure to keep an eye on the cupcakes during baking, as they may bake faster since there will be less batter in the liners. Allow the cupcakes to cool completely before decorating. (Note that you can save the balls or squares and reuse them for additional projects.)

Working with Candy Melts

For the projects in this book, I use candy melts in place of chocolate. Candy melts have a similar look and taste to chocolate, but they are very different to work with. Melting chocolate properly requires a process called *tempering*, which ensures the chocolate will harden with a crisp, glossy finish. Tempering involves temperature precision and a candy thermometer to do it properly. Conversely, candy melts are easier to use as they don't require tempering; you can just melt them and use them straightaway. They are also much more affordable than chocolate and come in a variety of colors.

Melting Candy Melts

To use candy melts, you can melt them in the microwave or over a double boiler.

For the microwave, add the candy melts to a microwave-safe bowl and heat them on 50 percent power for 1 minute. Stir thoroughly and then return to the microwave and heat in 30 second bursts at 50 percent power until the candy is melted.

For the double boiler, fill a small pan with about 1 inch (2.5cm) of water and bring it to a simmer over medium heat. Place a large heatproof bowl on top of the pan. (Make sure the bowl is large enough that it rests on the edges of the pan and not in the pan.) Add the candy melts to the bowl, reduce the heat to low, and stir continuously with a rubber spatula until the candy is melted. (The steam from the boiling water will melt the candy.)

If the candy is still too thick after it's melted, I highly recommend using a thinning aid that you can purchase with the candy melts from a cake decorating supply store or online. (Wilton EZ Thin dipping aid is a good option.) You can also add a small amount of vegetable shortening to thin it out. To reuse the candy melts, just let them set and keep them in an airtight container until ready to use.

Coloring Candy Melts

You can purchase most candy melts already colored; however, if you want to achieve a different color than what is available, you can melt different colors together. To color white candy melts, add a small amount of food coloring to the melted candy and then mix with a spatula. Continue adding food coloring in small amounts until you have the desired shade. Note that you must use oil-based food colors only; water-based food coloring will cause the candy to seize or harden.

To transfer the melted candy to a piping bag, place the piping bag inside a tall cup or glass, fold the top of the piping bag over the edges of the glass, then pour the melted chocolate into the piping bag. (Only fill the bag up to two-thirds full so you have room to close it.) The candy can set fast in the bag, which means you may need to keep putting it into the microwave to remelt it.

chapter 2

Buttercream
& CUPCAKE RECIPES

Vanilla and Flavored Cupcakes 24

Chocolate Cupcakes. 25

Red Velvet Cupcakes 26

Peanut Butter and Jelly Cupcakes . 27

Carrot Cupcakes. 28

Lemon Cupcakes 29

Rainbow Cupcakes 30

Chai Latte Cupcakes. 31

Cookie Dough Cupcakes. 32

Basic Buttercream 33

Chocolate Buttercream. 34

Oreo Buttercream. 34

Swiss Meringue Buttercream. 35

Cream Cheese Buttercream 36

Hybrid Buttercream 36

Black Buttercream 37

Vanilla and Flavored Cupcakes

Prep time

15 minutes

Baking time

20–22 minutes

Makes

12 cupcakes

150g (5.25oz) caster sugar

150g (5.25oz) self-rising flour

150g (5.25oz) unsalted butter (room temperature)

3 large eggs (room temperature)

1 tsp vanilla extract

1. Preheat the oven to 350°F (175°C) or 320°F (160°C) for a fan-forced oven. Line a 12-cup cupcake pan with 12 liners.

2. Sift the caster sugar and self-rising flour into the bowl of a stand mixer fitted with a paddle attachment. Add the butter and eggs. Mix on low until combined and then increase the speed to medium and beat for 30 seconds.

3. Stop the mixer and scrape down the sides of the bowl with a rubber spatula. Add the vanilla extract and beat on medium speed for another 30 seconds.

4. Divide the mixture between the 12 cupcake liners. (They should be three-quarters full.) Transfer to the oven and bake for 20 to 22 minutes or until a toothpick inserted into the center of a cupcake comes out clean.

variations

Flavored Cupcakes: Follow the recipe for the Vanilla Cupcakes, but swap out the vanilla extract for an equal amount of any flavored extract of your choice.

Funfetti Cupcakes: Follow the recipe for the Vanilla Cupcakes, but before adding the batter to the cupcake liners, gently fold 30g (1oz) of long rainbow sprinkles into the batter.

Chocolate Chip Cupcakes: Follow the recipe for the Vanilla Cupcakes, but before adding the batter to the cupcake liners, gently fold 150g (5.25oz) of chocolate chips into the batter.

Strawberry Jam Cupcakes: Follow the recipe for the Vanilla Cupcakes, but before adding the batter to the cupcake liners, gently fold 150g (5.25oz) of seedless strawberry jam into the batter.

Nutella Swirl Cupcakes: Follow the recipe for the Vanilla Cupcakes. Heat 75g (2.65oz) of Nutella in the microwave just long enough that it is pourable. Add 1 teaspoon of the Nutella to the top of each cupcake, and use a toothpick to swirl it through the batter.

Chocolate Cupcakes

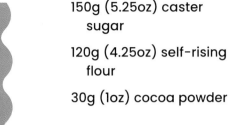

Prep time

20 minutes

Baking time

20–22 minutes

Makes

12 cupcakes

150g (5.25oz) caster sugar

120g (4.25oz) self-rising flour

30g (1oz) cocoa powder

150g (5.25oz) unsalted butter (room temperature)

3 large eggs (room temperature)

150g (5.25oz) milk chocolate chips

1. Preheat the oven to 350ºF (175ºC) or 320ºF (160ºC) for a fan-forced oven. Line a 12-cup cupcake pan with 12 liners.

2. Sift the caster sugar, self-rising flour, and cocoa powder into the bowl of a stand mixer fitted with a paddle attachment. Add the butter and eggs. Mix on low until combined and then increase the speed to medium and beat for 30 seconds.

3. Stop the mixer and scrape down the sides of the bowl with a rubber spatula. Continue beating on medium speed for another 30 seconds and then fold in the chocolate chips using a rubber spatula.

4. Divide the mixture between the 12 cupcake liners. (They should be three-quarters full.) Transfer to the oven and bake for 20 to 22 minutes or until a toothpick inserted into the center of a cupcake comes out clean.

Red Velvet Cupcakes

Prep time

20 minutes

Baking time

20–22 minutes

Makes

12 cupcakes

120g (4.25oz) self-rising flour

10g (0.35oz) cocoa powder

120g (4.25oz) caster sugar

½ tsp salt

130g (4.5oz) unsalted butter (room temperature)

2 large eggs (room temperature)

2 tbsp buttermilk

1 tsp vanilla extract

½ tsp red food coloring gel

½ tsp baking soda

1 tsp apple cider vinegar

1. Preheat the oven to 350ºF (175ºC) or 320ºF (160ºC) for a fan-forced oven. Line a 12-cup cupcake pan with 12 liners.

2. Sift the flour, cocoa powder, caster sugar, and salt into the bowl of a stand mixer fitted with a paddle attachment.

3. Add the butter and the eggs. Mix on low to combine and then increase the speed to medium for 1 minute. Stop the mixer and use a rubber spatula to scrape down the sides of the bowl.

4. Add the buttermilk, vanilla extract, and the red food coloring gel to the bowl. Mix on medium speed for another 20 seconds, and stop the mixer.

5. In a small bowl, combine the baking soda and vinegar and stir. When it begins to fizz, pour it into the flour mixture. Mix on low speed for another 20 seconds.

6. Stop the mixer and use a rubber spatula to scrape down the sides of the bowl. (If all the ingredients are not fully incorporated, mix by hand until they are fully incorporated.)

7. Divide the mixture between the 12 cupcake liners. (They should be three-quarters full.) Transfer to the oven and bake for 20 to 22 minutes or until a toothpick inserted into the center of a cupcake comes out clean.

Peanut Butter and Jelly Cupcakes

Prep time

20 minutes

Baking time

20–22 minutes

Makes

12 cupcakes

150g (5.25oz) caster sugar

150g (5.25oz) self-rising flour

½ tsp baking soda

150g (5.25oz) unsalted butter (room temperature)

3 large eggs (room temperature)

100g (3.5oz) smooth peanut butter

3 tbsp whole milk

100g (3.5oz) seedless strawberry jam, for decorating

1. Preheat the oven to 350ºF (175ºC) or 320ºF (160ºC) for a fan-forced oven. Line a 12-cup cupcake pan with 12 liners.

2. Sift the caster sugar, self-rising flour, and baking soda into the bowl of a stand mixer fitted with a paddle attachment. Add the butter, eggs, and peanut butter. Mix on low to combine and then increase the speed to medium and beat for 30 seconds.

3. Stop the mixer and scrape down the sides of the bowl with a rubber spatula. Add the milk and beat on medium speed for another 30 seconds.

4. Divide the mixture between the 12 cupcake liners. (They should be three-quarters full.) Transfer to the oven and bake for 20 to 22 minutes or until a toothpick inserted into the center of a cupcake comes out clean. Transfer the cupcakes to a wire rack to cool fully.

5. Once the cupcakes are cooled, use the large end of a piping tip or an apple corer to scoop out a hole from the center of each cupcake. (Keep the piece of cake to pop back on the top.) Fill the hole three-quarters full with strawberry jam, and push the piece of cake on top of the jam.

Carrot Cupcakes

Prep time

15 minutes

Baking time

18–20 minutes

Makes

12 cupcakes

2 large eggs (room temperature)

115g (4oz) granulated sugar

1 tsp vanilla extract

110ml (3.75fl oz) whole milk

110ml (3.75fl oz) vegetable oil

2 large carrots, grated (160g)

180g (6.25oz) self-rising flour

2 tsp baking powder

2 tsp ground cinnamon

¼ tsp ground nutmeg (optional)

½ cup chopped walnuts (optional)

1. Preheat the oven to 350ºF (175ºC) or 320ºF (160ºC) for a fan-forced oven. Line a 12-cup cupcake pan with 12 liners.

2. Add the eggs, granulated sugar, and vanilla extract to a large bowl. Whisk to combine. Add the milk and vegetable oil, and whisk again.

3. Gently stir in the grated carrots. (I find using a rubber spatula helps with this step.)

4. Add the self-rising flour, baking powder, cinnamon, and nutmeg (if using). Stir until combined. Fold in the walnuts (if using).

5. Divide the mixture between the 12 cupcake liners. (They should be two-thirds full.) Bake for 18 to 20 minutes or until a toothpick inserted into the center of a cupcake comes out clean.

Lemon Cupcakes

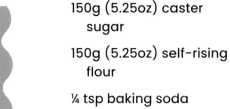

Prep time

20 minutes

Baking time

20–22 minutes

Makes

12 cupcakes

150g (5.25oz) caster sugar

150g (5.25oz) self-rising flour

¼ tsp baking soda

3 large eggs (room temperature)

150g (5.25oz) unsalted butter (room temperature)

Zest and juice of 1 lemon (about 3 tablespoons)

1. Preheat the oven to 350ºF (175ºC) or 320ºF (160ºC) for a fan-forced oven. Line a 12-cup cupcake pan with 12 liners.

2. Sift the caster sugar, self-rising flour, and baking soda into the bowl of a stand mixer fitted with the paddle attachment. Add the eggs and butter and mix on low until the ingredients are combined and then increase the speed to medium and beat for 30 seconds.

3. Stop the mixer and scrape down the sides of the bowl with a rubber spatula. Add the lemon zest and lemon juice. Beat on medium speed for another 30 seconds.

4. Divide the mixture between the 12 cupcake liners. (They should be three-quarters full.) Transfer to the oven and bake for 20 to 22 minutes or until a toothpick inserted into the center of a cupcake comes out clean.

Rainbow Cupcakes

Prep time

40 minutes

Baking time

20–22 minutes

Makes

12 cupcakes

170g (6oz) caster sugar

170g (6oz) self-rising flour

170g (6oz) unsalted butter (room temperature)

3 large eggs (room temperature)

1 tsp vanilla extract

Rainbow food coloring gels (red, orange, yellow, green, blue, and purple)

1. Preheat the oven to 350°F (175°C) or 320°F (160°C) for a fan-forced oven. Line a 12-cup cupcake pan with 12 liners.

2. Sift the caster sugar and self-rising flour into the bowl of a stand mixer fitted with a paddle attachment. Add the butter and eggs. Mix on low to combine, then increase the speed to medium and beat for 30 seconds.

3. Stop the mixer and scrape down the sides of the bowl with a rubber spatula. Add the vanilla extract and beat on medium speed for another 30 seconds.

4. Divide the batter equally into six separate bowls. Add a few drops of each food coloring gel into each bowl. Using separate spoons, gently mix the batter and food coloring gels together while trying not to incorporate too much air into the mixtures.

5. Add a spoonful of each colored batter to each cupcake liner, starting with the purple batter and working backward through the rainbow until you finish with the red batter. (The liners should be three-quarters full.)

6. Transfer to the oven and bake for 20 to 22 minutes or until a toothpick inserted into the center of a cupcake comes out clean.

Chai Latte Cupcakes

Prep time

20 minutes

Baking time

20–22 minutes

Makes

12 cupcakes

150g (5.25oz) caster sugar

150g (5.25oz) self-rising flour

3 tsp Chai Spice Mix

150g (5.25oz) unsalted butter (room temperature)

3 large eggs (room temperature)

1 tsp vanilla extract

FOR THE CHAI SPICE MIX:

1 tsp cardamom

2 tsp ground cinnamon

1 tsp ground ginger

1 tsp ground allspice

1. Preheat the oven to 350°F (175°C) or 320°F (160°C) for a fan-forced oven. Line a 12-cup cupcake pan with 12 liners.

2. Make the Chai Spice Mix by combining the spices in a small bowl. Mix the spices together.

3. Sift the sugar, flour, and 3 teaspoons of the Chai Spice Mix into the bowl of a stand mixer fitted with the paddle attachment. Add the butter and eggs. Mix on low to combine and then turn the speed up to medium and beat for 30 seconds.

4. Stop the mixer and scrape down the sides of the bowl with a rubber spatula. Add the vanilla extract and beat on medium speed for 30 seconds more.

5. Divide the mixture between the 12 cupcake liners. (They should be three-quarters full.) Transfer to the oven and bake for 20 to 22 minutes or until a toothpick inserted into the center of a cupcake comes out clean.

The Chai Spice Mix yields 5 teaspoons. If desired, the remaining 2 teaspoons can be added to a batch of buttercream to go with these cupcakes. However, the spices will tint the buttercream slightly, so only add the mix to a buttercream for a design that doesn't require a white buttercream.

Cookie Dough Cupcakes

Prep time

30 minutes (plus freezer time)

Baking time

20–22 minutes

Makes

12 cupcakes

FOR THE COOKIE DOUGH:

120g (4.25oz) unsalted butter (room temperature)

100g (3.5oz) caster sugar

50g (1.75oz) light brown sugar

100g (3.5oz) all-purpose flour

50g (1.75oz) milk chocolate chips

1 tsp vanilla extract

1 tbsp whole milk

Pinch of salt

FOR THE CUPCAKES:

125g (4.5oz) caster sugar

125g (4.5oz) self-rising flour

125g (4.5oz) unsalted butter (room temperature)

2 large eggs (room temperature)

1 tsp vanilla extract

50g (1.75oz) milk chocolate chips

1. To make the cookie dough, combine all the ingredients in the bowl of a stand mixer. Mix on low until combined into a dough. Roll the dough into 12 balls, each approximately 25g (0.875oz) in weight. (You will have some leftover dough.) Put the balls on a parchment-lined baking sheet and transfer them to the freezer to set for 2 to 3 hours.

2. When the setting time for the cookie dough balls is nearly complete, preheat the oven to 350ºF (175ºC) or 320ºF (160ºC) for a fan-forced oven. Line a 12-cup cupcake pan with 12 liners.

3. Sift the caster sugar and self-rising flour into the bowl of a stand mixer fitted with the paddle attachment. Add the butter and eggs and mix on low until all the ingredients are combined and then increase the speed to medium and beat for 30 seconds.

4. Stop the mixer and scrape down the sides of the bowl with a rubber spatula. Add the vanilla extract and chocolate chips and beat on medium speed for 30 seconds more.

5. Remove the cookie dough balls from the freezer and put one into each cupcake liner.

6. Divide the cupcake mixture between the 12 cupcake liners, adding it on top of the cookie dough balls. Transfer the cupcakes to the oven and bake for 20 to 22 minutes.

Basic Buttercream

250g (8.75oz) unsalted butter
(room temperature)

500g (17.5oz) confectioners' sugar,
divided

1 tbsp vanilla extract

2 tbsp heavy cream

1. Add the butter to the bowl of a stand mixer with a paddle attachment. Beat the butter on high speed for 5 minutes. Stop the mixer and use a rubber spatula to scrape down the sides of the bowl. Mix on medium for another 5 minutes. (The butter should now be much lighter in color.)

2. Sift half of the confectioners' sugar into the bowl and mix on low until combined. Add the vanilla extract and heavy cream and then sift in the remaining confectioners' sugar. Mix on low until combined. Stop the mixer and scrape down the sides of the bowl with a rubber spatula. Continue beating the mixture on medium until smooth.

3. Use a rubber spatula to push the buttercream back and forth around the sides of the bowl until any air bubbles have been removed.

If desired, replace the vanilla extract with an equal amount of flavored extract of your choice.

For **Bright White Buttercream**, replace the vanilla extract with an equal amount of clear vanilla extract. You can also use white food coloring to help whiten your buttercream, but for a large batch I find that you need to use a lot, and it can change the taste and texture of the finished product. Alternatively, you can add a tiny amount of violet or purple food coloring gel to your buttercream to help eliminate the yellow. (Purple and yellow are opposites on the color wheel, so they cancel each other out.) Be careful to only add the smallest amount, as too much will turn your buttercream gray. (I recommend using a toothpick to add the coloring.)

Chocolate Buttercream

250g (8.75oz) unsalted butter
(room temperature)

450g (16oz) confectioners' sugar, divided

50g (1.75oz) cocoa powder

3 tbsp heavy cream

1 tbsp vanilla extract

1. Add the butter to the bowl of a stand mixer fitted with a paddle attachment. Beat the butter on high speed for 5 minutes. Use a spatula to scrape down the sides of the bowl.

2. Sift in 225g (8oz) of the confectioners' sugar and the cocoa powder. Mix on low until combined, then add the heavy cream and vanilla extract and sift in the remaining 225g (8oz) of confectioners' sugar. Mix on low until combined. Stop the mixer and scrape down the sides of the bowl, then beat the mixture on medium until smooth.

3. Use a rubber spatula to push the buttercream back and forth around the sides of the bowl to eliminate air bubbles.

Oreo Buttercream

250g (8.75oz) unsalted butter, softened

500g (17.5oz) confectioners' sugar, divided

120ml (4fl oz) heavy cream, divided

1 tbsp vanilla extract

10 Oreo cookies

1. Add the butter to the bowl of a stand mixer fitted with a paddle attachment. Beat the butter on high for 5 minutes, then use a spatula to scrape down the sides of the bowl. Mix on medium for another 5 minutes. (The butter should become lighter in color.)

2. Sift 250g (8.75oz) of the confectioners' sugar into the bowl and mix on low until combined. Add 60ml of the heavy cream and the vanilla extract, then sift in the remaining 250g (8.75oz) of confectioners' sugar. Mix on low until just combined, then scrape down the sides of the bowl and beat the mixture on medium until smooth.

3. Add the Oreos to a food processor and process until a fine crumblike texture is achieved. (Alternatively, you can use a sharp knife to chop the cookies into crumbs. The smaller the crumbs, the easier the buttercream will be to work with.)

4. Add the crumbs to the bowl with the buttercream and mix on low. Gradually add in the remaining 60ml of heavy cream and continue mixing until you have the desired consistency. (Don't over mix, as the buttercream can turn gray!)

Swiss Meringue Buttercream

6 large egg whites (approximately 230g [8oz])

400g (14oz) granulated sugar

350g (12.25oz) unsalted butter, softened but still cool, cut into small chunks

2 tsp vanilla extract

¼ tsp salt

1. Add the egg whites and sugar to a large heat-safe bowl.

2. Fill a saucepan with 2 inches (5cm) of water. Bring to a simmer over medium heat.

3. Place the bowl with the egg and sugar mixture on top of the saucepan. (Don't let the bottom of the bowl touch the water.) Whisk the egg whites and sugar constantly for about 4 minutes or until the temperature reaches 160ºF (70ºC) on a thermometer. (You can also check by rubbing the mixture between your fingertips to make sure that the sugar is fully dissolved.)

4. Remove the bowl from the heat. Pour the mixture into the bowl of a stand mixer, fitted with a whisk attachment. Mix on medium–high speed for around 10 minutes or until stiff, glossy peaks form. (If the mixture is too warm and isn't whipping properly, transfer it to the fridge for 10 minutes and then return the bowl to the stand mixer and continue to mix until stiff peaks form.) Continue this step until the meringue is cool enough to add the butter (around 70ºF [20ºC]).

5. Switch the whisk attachment to the paddle attachment. Scrape down the sides and the bottom of the bowl with a rubber spatula.

6. Turn the stand mixer on to a medium-low speed and add one piece of butter at a time. Let each piece fully mix in before adding the next. When all the butter is fully mixed in, add the vanilla extract and salt. Continue mixing on low speed until the buttercream is silky smooth.

Before making this recipe, thoroughly clean any tools that will touch the meringue by wiping them with lemon juice or white vinegar.

Any grease or fat on the tools can make it difficult for the meringue to set.

Cream Cheese Buttercream

350g (12.25oz) unsalted butter
  (room temperature)

900g (32oz) confectioners' sugar, divided

1 tbsp vanilla extract

½ tsp salt

2 tbsp heavy cream

113g (4oz) cream cheese
  (block-style, not spread)

1. Add the butter to the bowl of a stand mixer fitted with a paddle attachment. Beat on medium speed for 10 minutes or until pale in color.

2. Sift 450g (16oz) of the confectioners' sugar into the bowl and then add the vanilla and salt. Mix on medium until the ingredients are incorporated. Sift in the remaining 450g (16oz) of confectioners' sugar and then add the cream. Mix for another 5 minutes on medium.

3. Stop the mixer and scrape down the sides of the bowl with a rubber spatula. Add the cream cheese and mix on low until you achieve a smooth consistency.

Hybrid Buttercream

150g (5.25oz) pasteurized egg whites
  from a carton (room temperature)

500g (17.5oz) confectioners' sugar

400g (14oz) unsalted butter, softened
  but still cool, cut into small chunks

2 tsp vanilla extract or flavoring
  of choice

½ tsp fine salt

1. Add the egg whites and confectioners' sugar to the bowl of a stand mixer. Using the whisk attachment, mix on low speed until the ingredients are combined.

2. Scrape down the sides of the bowl, increase the speed to high, and continue whisking for 5 to 10 minutes or until the mixture begins to develop stiff peaks.

3. Switch the whisk attachment to the paddle attachment. Add the butter, one chunk at a time, while mixing on low until all the butter is incorporated. Scrape down the sides of the bowl. Continue mixing on a low-medium speed for another 10 minutes.

4. Add the vanilla extract and salt, and mix on low until you achieve a smooth consistency.

5. Use a rubber spatula to push the buttercream back and forth around the sides of the bowl to eliminate air bubbles.

Black Buttercream

250g (8.75oz) unsalted butter (room temperature)

450g (16oz) confectioners' sugar, divided

50g (1.75oz) black cocoa powder

1 tsp vanilla extract

3 tbsp heavy cream

70g (2.5oz) dark chocolate

½ tsp black gel food coloring (optional)

1. Add the butter to the bowl of a stand mixer fitted with a paddle attachment. Beat on high speed for 5 minutes or until it is light in color. Sift in 225g (8oz) of the confectioners' sugar along with the black cocoa powder. Mix on low until all ingredients are incorporated.

2. Use a spatula to scrape the sides and the bottom of the bowl. Add the vanilla and heavy cream and then sift in the remaining 225g (8oz) of confectioners' sugar. Mix on low until all the ingredients are combined. Scrape down the sides of the bowl again.

3. Add the dark chocolate to a microwave-safe bowl and heat in 30 second bursts until the chocolate is melted. Allow it to cool for 10 minutes, and mix it in with the other ingredients on low speed until the ingredients are fully incorporated and the desired consistency is reached.

4. If the color of the buttercream is not dark enough, add the black gel food coloring and mix it on low. (The color develops over time, so be careful not to add more than is needed. I recommend making this the day before decorating to allow the color to intensify.)

5. Use a rubber spatula to push the buttercream back and forth around the sides of the bowl to eliminate air bubbles.

chapter 3

Holidays

Love Hearts 40

Love Monsters 43

Shamrocks 47

Pots of Gold .51

Bunny Butts 54

Easter Chicks 56

Bird Nests 59

Easter Baskets 63

Mister Brain 66

Spooky Skulls 69

Witches' Hats 73

Ghosts 77

Turkeys 81

Oh My, Pumpkin Pies! 85

Shaped Christmas Trees 89

Snow-Covered Christmas Trees . . . 93

Frosty and Friends (Snowmen) 97

Santas 101

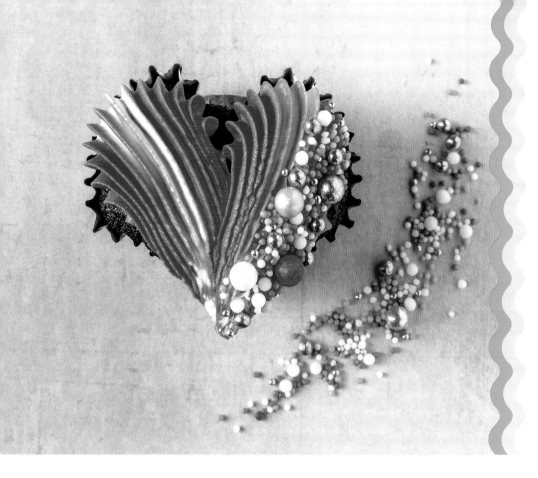

Prep time
40 minutes

Baking time
20 minutes

Decorating time
30 minutes

Makes
12 cupcakes

Love Hearts

Show your loved ones how much you care with these love heart cupcakes. You can make these with a multicolored buttercream as suggested or mix it up by coloring them all individually. A fancy alternative to the sprinkle decoration is using gold leaf as a finishing touch, which could be a special addition for a wedding or bridal shower.

EQUIPMENT

12-cup cupcake pan

12 foil cupcake liners

1 piping bag

1 large open star piping tip (8B)

36 foil squares

Tweezers

INGREDIENTS

12 Red Velvet Cupcakes (p. 26)

1 batch Hybrid Buttercream (p. 36)

Food coloring (pink, red)

Colored sprinkles

Prep and Baking

1. Roll 12 of the foil squares into balls. Fold the remaining 24 foil squares in half 4 times each to make smaller, sturdier squares.

2. Make the cupcake batter per the recipe instructions. Line a 12-cup cupcake pan with foil liners. Fill the liners half full with cupcake batter. Insert a foil ball at the top of each cupcake, and add two foil squares to the bottom of the liners to create the points of the hearts. Pinch the corners of the liners at the tops and bottoms to help the cupcakes keep their shapes while baking. Bake as instructed and allow to cool completely before decorating. *(see Photo 1)*

1

3. Make a batch of Hybrid Buttercream per the recipe instructions. Separate the buttercream into three equal-size batches. Color one batch red, one batch pink, and leave the third batch uncolored. Add the three colors to a piece of cling film, roll the buttercreams into a sausage, cut off one end, then add it to a piping bag fitted with piping tip 8B. (See "Piping a Multicolored Swirl" on page 19.) Secure the bag with a clip.

2

Decorating

1. Use the multicolored buttercream to pipe the hearts. Starting at the top left-hand side of the cupcake, hold the bag at an angle with the tip slightly above the surface of the cupcake, then squeeze the bag, lift, and gradually release the pressure as you pull the buttercream toward the bottom of the heart. *(see Photo 2)*

3

2. Repeat the process, this time going in the opposite direction. The two tails should overlap to create a point. *(see Photo 3)*

4

3. Pour the sprinkles into a small bowl. Hold a cupcake over the bowl at a slight angle and use a spoon to pour the sprinkles over one side of the buttercream heart. (The excess sprinkles will fall back into the bowl.) *(see Photo 4)*

4. Using tweezers, add larger sprinkles to the buttercream. *(see Photo 5)*

5

Love Monsters

These lovable monsters are perfect for Valentine's Day and can be made without the Oreo mouths, if preferred. Instead of cutting the lid from the cupcake, just leave the dome tops on and decorate in the same way. Or, change the color of the buttercream to orange or green, add some teeth, and you have a cute Halloween idea. Maybe your own little monster would love them for their birthday!

Prep time
40 minutes

Baking time
20 minutes

Decorating time
40 minutes

Makes
12 cupcakes

EQUIPMENT

12-cup cupcake pan

12 cupcake liners

3 piping bags

1 small round piping tip (12)

1 large open star piping tip (1M)

1 grass piping tip (233)

Serrated knife

INGREDIENTS

12 Rainbow Cupcakes (colored red) (p. 30)

1 batch Basic Buttercream (p. 33)

Red food coloring

6 Oreo cookies

12 large candy eyes

12 small candy eyes

12 strawberry Pocky Sticks

24 love heart sprinkles

Prep and Baking

1. Make the cupcake batter per the recipe instructions. Fill the cupcake liners about three-quarters full with batter. Bake the cupcakes as instructed and allow to cool completely. Once cooled, place the cupcakes in the fridge to chill for 30 minutes. (It's easier to slice the cupcakes when they are chilled.)

2. Once the cupcakes are chilled, use a serrated knife to slice the domes off the tops. Set them aside until you're ready to decorate.

3. Make a batch of Basic Buttercream per the recipe instructions. Color the buttercream red and add a small amount to a piping bag fitted with piping tip 12. Divide the remaining buttercream into two piping bags: one fitted with piping tip 2A and the other fitted with piping tip 233. Secure the bags with clips.

Decorating

1. Use the red buttercream and piping tip 1M to pipe a swirl of buttercream onto the bottom half of each cupcake. Hold the piping bag upright above the center of the cupcake and pipe a swirl, leaving a ¼-inch (0.5cm) gap around the edge. *(see Photo 1)*

2. Separate the Oreos into two halves and remove the cream filling. Use a serrated knife to carefully saw each half into two equal-size pieces. *(see Photo 2)*

1

2

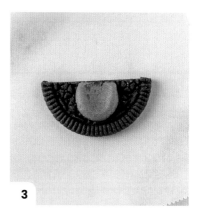

3

4

3. Use the red buttercream and piping tip 12 to add a tongue. Pipe a small dot of red buttercream in the center of the Oreo half, then use the large end of a small piping tip to spread the dot toward the cut edge of the Oreo. *(see Photo 3)*

4. Position the Oreo on the front of the cupcake, leaning it against the buttercream swirl to secure it in place. *(see Photo 4)*

5

5. Set the cupcake lid on top of the cupcake. (The front part of the lid should be resting on top of the Oreo, with the rest of the lid leaning back onto the buttercream swirl.) *(see Photo 5)*

6. Use the red buttercream and piping tip 233 to add the fur to the lid. Starting at the edge of the cupcake, hold the piping bag so that the tip is just above the cupcake. Squeeze some buttercream onto the surface, lift, release the pressure, then pull away in different directions. Work your way around the edge, finishing in the center of the cupcake. *(see Photo 6)*

6

7. Add one large eye and one small eye to each cupcake. *(see Photo 7)*

8. Cut the Pocky Sticks to size and then add one behind each eye by gently pushing them into the cupcake lid to secure them in place. Add a small amount of buttercream to the back of each sprinkle heart, then stick them to the end of each Pocky Stick. *(see Photo 8)*

7

8

Shamrocks

Sláinte! Paint the town green for St Patrick's Day with these simple pretzel shamrocks. If you'd like to add some extra sparkle, swap the rainbow sprinkles for gold sprinkles. You also could use a multicolored buttercream swirl in green, white, and orange to represent the flag of Ireland.

Prep time

40 minutes

Baking time

20 minutes

Decorating time

1 hour

Makes

12 cupcakes

EQUIPMENT

12-cup cupcake pan

12 green cupcake liners

2 piping bags

1 large open star piping tip (1M)

Baking sheet

Parchment paper

Toothpicks

INGREDIENTS

12 Rainbow Cupcakes (colored green) (p. 30)

1 batch Basic Buttercream (p. 33)

Green food coloring

36 mini pretzels

340g (12oz) green candy melts

13 pretzel sticks

Small round rainbow sprinkles

Edible glitter (optional)

Prep and Baking

1. Line a baking sheet with parchment paper. Set aside.

2. Make the cupcake batter per the recipe instructions and then color the batter green. Fill the cupcake liners three-quarters full and bake as instructed. Allow the cupcakes to cool completely before decorating.

3. Make a batch of Basic Buttercream per the recipe instructions and then color the entire batch green. Transfer it to a piping bag fitted with piping tip 1M. Secure the bag with a clip.

4. Place the mini pretzels on the prepared baking sheet.

1

Decorating

1. Melt the green candy melts in a microwave-safe bowl. (See "Working with Candy Melts" on page 21.) Transfer the melted green chocolate to a piping bag and cut off the end of the bag. Fill the inside of each pretzel with the chocolate to create a heart shape, swirling the chocolate with a toothpick to level it out, if necessary. Sprinkle the small rainbow sprinkles over the top before the chocolate sets. *(see Photo 1)*

2. Cover one half of each pretzel stick with the melted green chocolate by holding the stick over parchment paper and drizzling the chocolate over the stick. Shake off any excess chocolate and then lay the sticks onto the prepared baking sheet to set. (The sticks can also be decorated with rainbow sprinkles.) Transfer the sheet to the fridge to allow the chocolate to set for 15 minutes. *(see Photo 2)*

2

3

3. Remove the baking sheet from the fridge and transfer the pretzels and sticks to a plate. Assemble the shamrocks by adding a large dot of green chocolate onto the parchment paper. Position the top of the pretzel stick in the middle of the chocolate and then add three pretzels around the stick. Discard the parchment paper and transfer the baking sheet to the fridge to allow the shamrocks to set for 15 minutes. *(see Photo 3)*

4. Use the green buttercream and piping tip 1M to pipe a swirl onto each cupcake. Hold the piping bag upright and just above the center of the cupcake. Squeeze out a dot of buttercream and then move the tip in a circle around the dot. Continue squeezing the bag while moving up in a spiral until you reach the desired height, ending the spiral at the center of the cupcake. Stop squeezing before pulling the tip away. *(see Photo 4)*

5. Use the spare pretzel stick to push a hole through the middle of the buttercream and into the cupcake. *(see Photo 5)*

6. Carefully remove the shamrocks from the parchment paper and insert them into the holes. Push them down very gently until they are secured in place. Sprinkle the edible glitter (if using) over the top. *(see Photo 6)*

4

5

6

Pots of Gold

If you can't find the end of a rainbow, you can make your own super cute pots of gold for a St. Patrick's Day celebration! Swap the rainbows and gold for some green sugar balls and candy eyes to turn this idea into witches' cauldrons for Halloween.

Prep time

1 hour

Baking time

20 minutes

Decorating time

30 minutes

Makes

12 cupcakes

EQUIPMENT

12-cup cupcake pan

12 foil cupcake liners

2 piping bags

1 jumbo round piping tip (809)

1 small round piping tip (10)

Baking sheet

Parchment paper

Palette knife (optional)

INGREDIENTS

12 Chocolate Cupcakes (p. 25)

1 batch Black Buttercream (p. 37)

3 rainbow belt candies (each cut into 4 pieces)

1 package gold sugar pearls

Edible glitter (optional)

Prep and Baking

1. Line a baking sheet with parchment paper. Set aside.

2. Make the cupcake batter per the recipe instructions. Line a 12-cup cupcake pan with foil cupcake liners. Fill the cups two-thirds full with cupcake batter. Bake as instructed and allow to cool completely before decorating.

3. Make a batch of Black Buttercream per the recipe instructions. Add one-third of the buttercream to a piping bag fitted with piping tip 10. Add the remaining buttercream to a piping bag fitted with piping tip 809. Secure the bags with clips.

1

Decorating

1. Use the Black Buttercream and piping tip 809 to pipe a dollop of the buttercream on top of the cupcakes. Hold the piping bag upright with the tip just above the center of the cupcake. Squeeze the bag and slowly pull upward. Release the pressure and pull away, leaving a gap around the edge to allow for spreading when pressed down. *(see Photo 1)*

2. Gently press the cupcakes face down onto the prepared baking sheet. Transfer the baking sheet to the freezer for 15 minutes or until the buttercream peels away from the parchment paper cleanly. (See "Using the Flip-and-Freeze Method" on page 18). Remove the baking sheet from the freezer and peel the cupcakes away from the parchment paper. *(see Photo 2)*

3. Starting three-quarters of the way up the cupcake, use the black buttercream and piping tip 10 to pipe a line from one side of the cupcake to the other. *(see Photo 3)*

2

3

4. Add a small amount of buttercream to the back of a piece of rainbow belt and secure it to the top left-hand side of the cupcake. *(see Photo 4)*

5. Arrange gold sugar pearls around the top part of the cupcake and the rainbow belt. (If needed, you can secure them by adding a small amount of buttercream to the pearls.) *(see Photo 5)*

6. Use the black buttercream and piping tip 10 to add feet to the pot of gold. Hold the piping bag at an angle with the tip touching the bottom outer part of the buttercream pot. Squeeze out a ball of buttercream and slowly pull away. Repeat this step on the other side. (You can smooth them out with a palette knife if they are too pointed at the bottom.) *(see Photo 6)*

7. Sprinkle the edible gold glitter over the top (if using). *(see Photo 7)*

4

5

6

7

Prep time

30 minutes

Baking time

20 minutes

Decorating time

40 minutes

Makes

12 cupcakes

Bunny Butts

Nothing says Easter quite like a treat made into a bunny butt! If you're not a fan of coconut, you can swap it out for white sprinkles or grated white candy melts. Alternatively, serve on a bed of coconut grass and crushed Oreos for a baby shower or an Earth Day celebration.

EQUIPMENT

12-cup cupcake pan

12 foil cupcake liners

2 piping bags

1 large round piping tip (1A)

12 foil balls

INGREDIENTS

12 Carrot Cupcakes (p. 28)

1 batch Cream Cheese Buttercream (p. 36)

Desiccated coconut

12 white marshmallows

50g (1.75oz) white fondant

100g (3.5oz) pink candy melts

Prep and Baking

1. Make the cupcake batter per the recipe instructions. Line a 12-cup cupcake pan with foil liners and fill the liners half full with batter. Insert a foil ball at the bottom of the cupcake liner to create the shape of the bunny butt. Bake as instructed and allow to cool completely before decorating. *(see Photo 1)*

2. Make a batch of Cream Cheese Buttercream per the recipe instructions. Transfer the buttercream to a piping bag fitted with piping tip 1A. Secure the bag with a clip.

Decorating

1. Use the Cream Cheese Buttercream to pipe the butt shapes onto the cupcakes. Starting at the bottom left, hold the bag upright, squeeze a dot, then pull the buttercream up and in, releasing the pressure at the top of the cupcake. Repeat the process going the opposite direction. (The buttercream will resemble an upside-down heart shape.) *(see Photo 2)*

2. Pour the desiccated coconut into a bowl. Gently press the buttercream into the coconut.

3. Cut the marshmallows in half and apply a small amount of buttercream to the sticky sides. Attach them to the bottoms of the cupcakes. *(see Photo 3)*

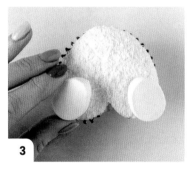

4. Heat the pink candy melts and transfer them to a piping bag. (See "Working with Candy Melts" on page 21.) Pipe the paw pads onto the marshmallows. *(see Photo 4)*

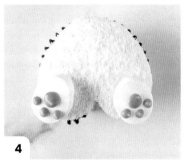

5. Roll out 12 equal-size balls of the white fondant that are about the size of a marble. Use a small amount of buttercream to attach them for the bunny tails. *(see Photo 5)*

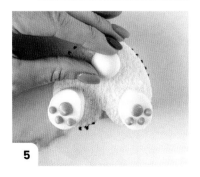

Prep time

40 minutes

Baking time

20 minutes

Decorating time

30 minutes

Makes

12 cupcakes

Easter Chicks

Treat your family and friends to these irresistible chick cupcakes. These adorable little treats are perfect for Easter, spring, or even a baby shower. Let the kids get creative with this simple and fun idea. These lovely lemony cupcakes topped with a delicious cream cheese buttercream are so tasty, you will need to make two batches!

EQUIPMENT

12-cup cupcake pan

12 foil cupcake liners

1 piping bag

1 large round piping tip (1A)

24 foil balls

Tweezers

INGREDIENTS

12 Lemon Cupcakes (p. 29)

1 batch Cream Cheese Buttercream (p. 36)

Yellow food coloring

Yellow sanding sugar

24 black round sprinkles

36 orange M&M's or Reese's Pieces

Prep and Baking

1. Make the cupcake batter per the recipe instructions. Line a 12-cup cupcake pan with foil cupcake liners and fill the liners half full with the cupcake batter. Insert a foil ball outside both sides of the liner and just above the halfway mark so the top half of the cupcake is slightly smaller than the bottom. Bake the cupcakes as instructed and allow to cool completely before decorating. *(see Photo 1)*

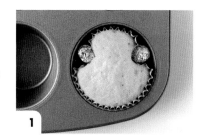

2. Make a batch of Basic Buttercream per the recipe instructions and color it yellow. Transfer the buttercream to a piping bag fitted with piping tip 1A. Secure the bag with a clip.

Decorating

1. Using the yellow buttercream, pipe the head of the chick by piping a large dot of buttercream in the center of the top part of the cupcake. Leave a ¼-inch (0.5cm) gap around the sides and at the top of the dot, as it will spread when it is pushed into the sanding sugar. *(see Photo 2)*

2. For the body, pipe a slightly larger circle of buttercream on the bottom part of the cupcake. Start at the top and pipe a swirl, finishing in the middle. Again, leave a ¼-inch (0.5cm) gap around the edges. *(see Photo 3)*

3. Pour the sanding sugar into a bowl. Press the buttercream into the sugar as gently as possible, trying to keep the shape of the chick as perfect as you can. *(see Photo 4)*

4. Use tweezers to add two black round sprinkles for the eyes. *(see Photo 5)*

5. Add an orange candy for the beak, then add two more orange candies for the feet. *(see Photo 6)*

Bird Nests

These bird nest cupcakes are a great way to add a whimsical touch to any springtime occasion. They're so cute and simple, the little bakers in your life will have a ball helping decorate these. Make a tray of chocolate nest cupcakes for Easter or spring birthday parties, or even just as an excuse to use all the mini eggs you have left over.

Prep time

40 minutes

Baking time

20 minutes

Decorating time

40 minutes

Makes

12 cupcakes

EQUIPMENT

12-cup cupcake pan

12 cupcake liners

3 piping bags

1 grass piping tip (233)

1 large round piping tip (1A)

1 small leaf piping tip (352)

INGREDIENTS

12 Carrot Cupcakes (p. 28)

1 batch Basic Buttercream (p. 33)

Yellow food coloring

40g (1.5oz) cocoa powder

2 tbsp heavy cream

18 mini eggs

Black and orange sprinkles

Prep and Baking

1. Make the cupcake batter per the recipe instructions. Line a 12-cup cupcake pan with cupcake liners and fill the liners two-thirds full with the cupcake batter. Bake as instructed and then allow to cool completely before decorating.

2. Make a batch of Basic Buttercream per the recipe instructions. Transfer a third of the buttercream to a separate bowl and color it yellow. Transfer half of the yellow buttercream to a piping bag fitted with piping tip 1A and the other half to a piping bag fitted with piping tip 352. Secure the bags with clips.

3. Add the cocoa powder and heavy cream to the remaining buttercream and mix until smooth. Transfer to a piping bag fitted with piping tip 233. Secure the bag with a clip.

Decorating

1. Use the chocolate buttercream to pipe the nests on all the cupcakes. Hold the piping bag upright and squeeze while moving around the cupcake in circles. Leave a gap in the center for the chicks and mini eggs. (Remember, real nests are far from perfect-looking, so just have fun while piping these!) *(see Photo 1)*

2. Add three mini eggs to the middle of six of the cupcakes and set them aside. *(see Photo 2)*

3. Using the yellow buttercream and piping tip 1A, pipe the chicks' bodies in the centers of the remaining cupcakes. Hold the piping bag upright and squeeze while slowly lifting the bag. *(see Photo 3)*

4. Pull away and repeat the process to create the chicks' heads, making the heads slightly smaller than the bodies. *(see Photo 4)*

5. Use tweezers to add black sprinkles for the eyes and an orange sprinkle for the beak. *(see Photo 5)*

6. Use the yellow buttercream and piping tip 352 to pipe two wings. Hold the piping bag at an angle with the tip touching the chick's body and then squeeze and pull away. Repeat on the opposite side. *(see Photo 6)*

Easter Baskets

Yes, you can eat the whole thing! Get egg-cited for Easter by making a cupcake tray full of these chocolate Easter baskets. If desired, top them with mini eggs along with cute little chicks and bunnies for that showstopping look. You could also top them with flowers for a gorgeous Mother's Day or garden-party theme.

Prep time

1 hour

Baking time

20 minutes

Decorating time

40 minutes

Makes

12 cupcakes

EQUIPMENT

12-cup cupcake pan

24 foil cupcake liners

2 piping bags

1 grass piping tip (233)

Baking sheet

Parchment paper

Small silicone brush

INGREDIENTS

12 Chocolate Cupcakes (p. 25)

1 batch Basic Buttercream (p. 33)

Green food coloring

400g (14oz) chocolate candy melts

36 mini chocolate eggs

Baking and Prep

1. Line a baking sheet with parchment paper. Set aside.

2. Make the cupcake batter per the recipe instructions. Place 12 foil liners in the cupcake pan and fill the liners three-quarters full with batter. Bake as instructed and allow to cool completely before removing the cupcakes from their liners and setting them aside.

3. Make a batch of Basic Buttercream per the recipe instructions and color it green. Transfer it to a piping bag fitted with piping tip 233. Secure the bag with a clip.

4. Melt the candy melts in a microwave-safe bowl. (See "Working with Candy Melts" on page 21.)

5. Create the basket handles by adding a small amount of the melted chocolate to the piping bag. Cut off the end of the bag and pipe 12 U shapes onto the baking sheet lined with parchment paper. (The handles should be slightly smaller than the width of a cupcake.) Transfer the tray to the fridge for 15 minutes to let them set. *(see Photo 1)*

6. Place the remaining foil liners in the cupcake pan. Pour about 1 tablespoon of the chocolate into the bottom of each liner and then use a silicone brush to spread the chocolate up the sides of the liner. Repeat until all the liners have a coating of chocolate. Let them sit at room temperature for about 30 minutes. Add a second coating of chocolate and then transfer the pan to the fridge until the chocolate is fully set, about 15 minutes. *(see Photo 2)*

7. Remove the cupcake pan from the fridge and carefully peel the liners away from the chocolate cases. Place the chocolate cupcakes into the chocolate cases. *(see Photo 3)*

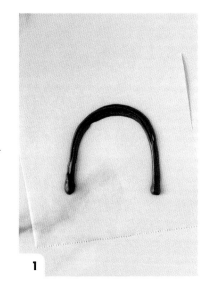

1

2

3

Decorating

1. Use the green buttercream to pipe grass onto the tops of the cupcakes. Begin by piping around the edges of a cupcake, working your way into the center. Hold the piping bag upright and just above the surface of the cupcake. Squeeze the bag and pull away in the direction that you want the grass to fall. (Remember to keep the piping close together so the cake doesn't show through.) *(see Photo 4)*

2. Set three mini chocolate eggs in the center of the grass for each cupcake. *(see Photo 5)*

3. Attach the handles by adding a small amount of melted chocolate to the ends of the handles and then attaching the handles to the chocolate cases. (If you have trouble keeping the handles in place, you can use toothpicks to hold them in place until the chocolate sets.) *(see Photo 6)*

4

5

6

Prep time

40 minutes

Baking time

20 minutes

Decorating time

40 minutes

Makes

12 cupcakes

Mister Brain

Have you got cupcakes on the brain? Or brains on your cupcakes? Wow your guests this Halloween with these scarily sweet treats. Make them green for zombie brains. Or, if you're feeling super gruesome, add a medicine syringe full of strawberry sauce onto the top of his brain!

EQUIPMENT

12-cup cupcake pan

12 cupcake liners

2 piping bags

1 large open star piping tip (1M)

1 small round piping tip (7)

Serrated knife

INGREDIENTS

12 Rainbow Cupcakes (colored pink) (p. 30)

1 batch Basic Buttercream (p. 33)

Pink food coloring gel

24 large candy eyes

Strawberry dessert sauce

Prep and Baking

1. Make the cupcake batter per the recipe instructions. Add about three drops of the pink food coloring to the batter, then stir to combine. Fill the cupcake liners about three-quarters full with the batter. Bake as instructed and allow to cool completely.

2. Once cooled, place the cupcakes in the fridge to chill for 30 minutes. (It's easier to slice the cupcakes when they are chilled.) Once the cupcakes are chilled, use a serrated knife to slice the domes off the tops of the cupcakes and then set the domes aside until you're ready to decorate.

3. Make a batch of Basic Buttercream per the recipe instructions. Color it pink with the pink food coloring. Divide the buttercream evenly into one bag fitted with piping tip 1M and another bag fitted with piping tip 7.

Decorating

1. Use the pink buttercream and piping tip 1M to pipe a swirl of buttercream on the bottom half of each cupcake. Hold the piping bag upright above the center of the cupcake and pipe a swirl, leaving a ¼-inch (0.5cm) gap around the edge. *(see Photo 1)*

2. Add two candy eyes to the buttercream at the front of the cupcake. (The back of the eyes should be touching the buttercream, which will secure them in place.) Place the dome of the cupcake on top of the buttercream, with the front part resting over the top of the eyes. *(see Photo 2)*

3. Use the other half of the pink buttercream and piping tip 7 to pipe the brain pattern on top of the cupcake lid. Start at the back of the lid, pipe a line down the center to the front of the cupcake and then back again. *(see Photo 3)*

4. Pipe squiggly back-and-forth lines on the rest of the lid to resemble a brain. *(see Photo 4)*

5. Drizzle a small amount of the strawberry sauce over the top of the brain design. *(see Photo 5)*

Spooky Skulls

Get into the Halloween spirit and whip up a batch of these spooktacular skull cupcakes, then watch with joy as your guests sink their teeth into these eerie treats! They're guaranteed to be the talk of the Halloween table. Add some color and turn this idea into sugar skulls for a Day of the Dead-themed celebration.

Prep time

40 minutes

Baking time

20 minutes

Decorating time

40 minutes

Makes

12 cupcakes

EQUIPMENT

12-cup cupcake pan

12 foil cupcake liners

2 piping bags

1 large round piping tip (2A)

Baking sheet

Parchment paper

24 foil balls

Palette knife

Dropper

Toothpick

INGREDIENTS

12 Red Velvet Cupcakes (p. 26)

1 batch Bright White Buttercream (p. 33)

Strawberry dessert sauce

20g (0.75oz) black candy melts

1   2   3

Prep and Baking

1. Line a baking sheet with parchment paper. Set aside.

2. Make the cupcake batter per the recipe instructions. Line a 12-cup cupcake pan with foil liners and fill the liners half full with batter. Insert a foil ball at both sides of the liners to create skull shapes. Pinch the corners of the liners to keep the shapes while the cupcakes are baking. Bake as instructed and allow to cool completely before decorating. *(see Photo 1)*

3. Make a batch of Bright White Buttercream per the recipe instructions. Transfer the buttercream to a piping bag fitted with piping tip 2A.

Decorating

1. Pipe the skull shapes onto the cupcakes. Pipe a circle for the top half of the skull and then a smaller square shape for the bottom half. Leave a ¼-inch (0.5cm) gap around the edge to allow room for spreading of the buttercream when it is pushed down. Smooth out the buttercream with a palette knife to fill in any gaps before pressing the cupcakes down onto the parchment paper. *(see Photo 2)*

4   **5**

2. Gently press the skulls down onto the prepared baking sheet. Transfer the tray to the freezer for 15 to 20 minutes. (See "Using the Flip-and-Freeze Method" on page 18.)

3. Transfer the cupcakes from the freezer to the fridge. (The buttercream needs to be cold for this step, so it's best to take one cupcake out of the fridge at a time.) Using the large end of a small piping tip, make eye holes in the buttercream. Hold the piping tip in place and gently rotate it to make a hole in the buttercream, pushing it down until it touches the cake and then lifting it out. (The buttercream should lift out with the tip, leaving perfect eye holes.) If the buttercream feels too stiff to work with, let it sit at room temperature for a few minutes. Repeat this step for all the cupcakes. *(see Photo 3)*

4. Heat the black candy melts and transfer the melted candy to a piping bag. (See "Working with Candy Melts" on page 21.) Cut a small hole in the end of the bag and pipe the nostrils and the mouth. *(see Photo 4)*

5. Use a dropper to fill the eye holes with strawberry sauce and then use a toothpick to drag some of the sauce out of the eye holes to give the eyes a bleeding effect. *(see Photo 5)*

Witches' Hats

Ding dong! The wicked witch . . . has lost her hat! You can make these hats as tall or as small as you like by simply adding more or less chocolate onto the sugar cones. Change the color of the candy melts to green and add large colored sugar balls to create fabulous Christmas tree toppers.

Prep time

1 hour

Baking time

20 minutes

Decorating time

1 hour

Makes

12 cupcakes

EQUIPMENT

12-cup cupcake pan

12 cupcake liners

2 piping bags

1 large open star piping tip (1M)

Baking sheet

Parchment paper

Wire cooling rack

Cling film

INGREDIENTS

12 Chai Latte Cupcakes (p. 31)

1 batch Swiss Meringue Buttercream (p. 35)

Food coloring (orange, yellow, purple)

12 sugar cones

340g (12oz) black candy melts

Black sanding sugar

Prep and Baking

1. Line a baking sheet with parchment paper and then set the wire cooling rack on top of the parchment paper. Set aside.

2. Make the cupcake batter per the recipe instructions. Line a 12-cup cupcake pan with cupcake liners and then fill the liners two-thirds full with the cupcake batter. Bake as instructed and then allow to cool completely before decorating.

3. Make a batch of Swiss Meringue Buttercream per the recipe instructions. Divide the buttercream into three equal-size portions. Color one portion orange, one portion yellow, and one portion purple. Add the three colors to a piece of cling film, roll the buttercreams into a sausage, cut off one end, then add it to a piping bag fitted with piping tip 1M. (See "Piping a Multicolored Swirl" on page 19.) Secure the bag with a clip.

Decorating

1. Working four at a time, begin making the hats by laying a piece of cling film on a flat surface and setting a sugar cone on top of the film with the pointed end at the very edge of the film. Fold the film over the cone to cover it. (Keep the cling film as neat as possible at the pointed end of the cone. The melted chocolate will seep into any creases, making it difficult to remove from the film when the chocolate has set.) *(see Photo 1)*

2. Twist the bottom end of the cling film and tuck it inside the cone. Place the covered cones onto the wire rack. *(see Photo 2)*

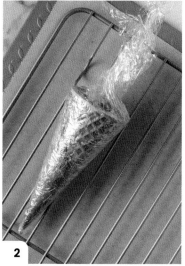

3. Melt the black candy melts in a microwave-safe bowl. (See "Working with Candy Melts" on page 21.) Transfer the melted candy to a piping bag and then cut off the end to make a small hole.

4. Drizzle the candy over the front half of the cone using a back-and-forth motion. Start at the largest end of the cone, approximately 2 inches (5cm) from the opening and move down to the point and back up again. Allow the candy to set and then repeat this step, adding another layer of candy drizzle to the cones. *(see Photo 3)*

5. Sprinkle the black sanding sugar over the candy and then transfer the hat tops to the fridge to set for 15 minutes.

4

6. Turn the hat tops over so that the candy-covered side is facing down on the wire rack. Repeat the coating process for the opposite side of the cone. Transfer the baking sheet to the fridge for 15 minutes to set.

7. When the candy has set, remove the baking sheet from the fridge. Untwist the bottom of the cling film, carefully remove the cone, and gently wiggle the cling film to release it from the candy and remove it. *(see Photo 4)*

5

8. Add a clean sheet of parchment paper to the baking sheet. Use the melted candy to pipe the bottoms of the hats onto the paper. Pipe a circle 2¼ inches (6cm) wide and then fill it in by piping the candy in a spiral motion. While the chocolate is still wet, sprinkle sanding sugar over the hat bottoms and then set the hat tops onto the centers of the hat bottoms to create the hats. Transfer the hats to the fridge to set. *(see Photo 5)*

6

9. Use the multicolored buttercream to pipe a swirl onto each cupcake. Hold the piping bag upright and just above the center of the cupcake. Squeeze out a dot of buttercream and then move the tip in a circle around the dot. Continue squeezing the bag while moving up in a spiral motion until you reach the desired height and then stop squeezing before pulling the tip away, ending the spiral at the center of the cupcake. *(see Photo 6)*

10. When the chocolate hats are set, remove them from the fridge and carefully lift them from the parchment paper. Sit them on top of the buttercream swirls. *(see Photo 7)*

7

Ghosts

No tricks, only treats with these boo-tiful ghost cupcakes! Your own little own "boos" will love making and eating these cuties for Halloween. You could swap the mini cupcake for candy corn or cute candy pumpkins. Give them all different expressions to mix things up.

Prep time

40 minutes

Baking time

20 minutes

Decorating time

40 minutes

Makes

12 cupcakes

EQUIPMENT

12-cup cupcake pan

12 foil cupcake liners

3 piping bags

1 large round piping tip (2A)

1 small round piping tip (10)

1 small open star piping tip (32)

12 foil balls

Palette knife

INGREDIENTS

12 Vanilla Cupcakes (p. 24)

1 batch Bright White Buttercream (p. 33)

Orange food coloring

20g (0.75oz) black candy melts

6 Reese's Minis, each cut in half

Mini colored sprinkles

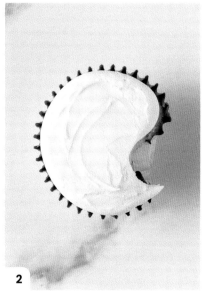

1

2

3

Prep and Baking

1. Line a baking sheet with parchment paper. Set aside.

2. Make the cupcake batter per the recipe instructions. Line a 12-cup cupcake pan with foil cupcake liners and fill the liners half full with batter. Insert a foil ball to the right-hand side of the liner to create a ghost shape. Pinch the tail parts of the liners into points. Bake as instructed and allow to cool completely. *(see Photo 1)*

3. Make a batch of Bright White Buttercream per the recipe instructions. Scoop out 1 cup of the buttercream and color it orange. Transfer the orange buttercream to a piping bag fitted with piping tip 32. Secure the bag with a clip.

4. Add one-third of the remaining white buttercream to a piping bag fitted with piping tip 10, then add the remaining buttercream to a piping bag fitted with piping tip 2A.

Decorating

1. Pipe the ghost shapes onto the cupcakes. Hold the piping bag with the white buttercream and piping tip 10 to the right side of the cupcake, starting at the tail. Pipe the outline of the ghost, finishing back at the tail. Pull away to the right to create a point. (Try not to go over the edges of the liner as the buttercream will spread when pushed onto the parchment paper.) Use the buttercream with piping tip 2A to fill in the middle of the ghost shape. Use a palette knife to smooth out the buttercream and fill in any gaps. *(see Photo 2)*

4 **5** **6**

2. Gently press the ghosts down onto the prepared baking sheet. Transfer the baking sheet to the freezer for 15 to 20 minutes. (See "Using the Flip-and-Freeze Method" on page 18.) Remove from the freezer and peel the cupcakes from the parchment paper.

3. Place half a Reese's Mini cut-side down onto the ghost's body, leaving enough room above the cup for the swirl on top and the ghost's face. *(see Photo 3)*

4. Use the white buttercream to pipe the arms. Hold the piping bag upright and just above one side of the Reese's Mini. Squeeze the bag and pull away to the edge of the ghost. Repeat this step for the opposite side. Use a spatula to smooth out the edges, if needed. *(see Photo 4)*

5. Use the orange buttercream and piping tip 32 to turn the Reese's Mini into a mini cupcake. Hold the piping bag at an angle with the tip just above one end of the Reese's Cup. Pipe a line back and forth, getting smaller each time, then pulling away at the top. Use tweezers to add some mini sprinkles to the cupcake. *(see Photo 5)*

6. Heat the black candy melts and transfer the melted candy to a piping bag. (See "Working with Candy Melts" on page 21.) Cut a small hole in the end of the bag and pipe the eyes and mouth. *(see Photo 6)*

Turkeys

Have some fun and make these colorful turkey cupcakes for Thanksgiving. With their adorable chocolate faces, they will be a huge hit with adults and kids alike. Try not to gobble them all up before your guests arrive!

Prep time

40 minutes

Baking time

20 minutes

Decorating time

40 minutes

Makes

12 cupcakes

EQUIPMENT

12-cup cupcake pan

12 foil cupcake liners

4 piping bags

3 small round piping tips (12)

1 small round piping tip (3)

24 foil squares

INGREDIENTS

12 Chocolate Cupcakes (p. 25)

1 batch Swiss Meringue Buttercream (p. 35)

Food coloring (red, yellow, orange)

12 Reese's Miniature Cups

24 candy eyes

6 orange mini M&M's, cut into halves

Prep and Baking

1. Make the cupcake batter per the recipe instructions. Insert rectangular, folded pieces of foil into the bottom corners of the cupcake to create a point. Pinch the cupcake liner into a point. Bake as instructed and allow to cool completely before decorating. *(see Photo 1)*

1

2. Make a batch of Swiss Meringue Buttercream per the recipe instructions. Divide the buttercream into three equal-size portions. Color one portion of the buttercream red and transfer a third of it to a piping bag fitted with piping tip 3. Add the remaining red buttercream to a piping bag fitted with piping tip 12. For the remaining two portions, color one portion yellow and one portion orange. Transfer the portions to separate piping bags each fitted with piping tip 12.

2

3

Decorating

1. Once the cupcakes have cooled, and with the pointed part of the cupcake at the bottom, use piping tip 12 and the red buttercream to pipe a row of dots across the top edge of the cupcake. *(see Photo 2)*

2. Use the large end of a piping tip to spread the dots into feathers. *(see Photo 3)*

3. Repeat the process with a row of orange dots and then yellow dots, working your way down to the point of the cupcake. *(see Photo 4)*

4. Add a small amount of buttercream to the top side of the Reese's Cup. Attach the Reese's, top side facing down, at the bottom of the feathers. *(see Photo 5)*

5. Use a small amount of melted candy to affix two candy eyes and half an orange M&M for the beak. *(see Photo 6)*

6. Use piping tip 3 and the red buttercream to pipe a wattle next to the beak. *(see Photo 7)*

4

5

6

7

Oh My, Pumpkin Pies!

Everyone loves pumpkin pie, right? Even if you're not a fan of pie, you can add a fun twist to your Thanksgiving dessert table with these impostor pies. They look like pies, but they taste like cupcakes!

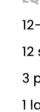

Prep time

30 minutes

Baking time

20 minutes

Decorating time

30 minutes

Makes

12 cupcakes

EQUIPMENT

12-cup cupcake pan

12 silver foil cupcake liners

3 piping bags

1 large open star piping tip (4B)

1 large round piping tip (1A)

1 small open star piping tip (18)

Baking sheet

Parchment paper

INGREDIENTS

12 Chai Latte Cupcakes (p. 31)

1 batch Hybrid Buttercream (p. 36)

Food coloring (orange, brown, yellow)

1

2

Prep and Baking

1. Line a baking sheet with parchment paper. Set aside.

2. Make the cupcake batter per the recipe instructions. Line a 12-cup cupcake pan with foil cupcake liners and then fill the liners two-thirds full with batter. Bake as instructed and allow to cool completely before decorating.

3. Make a batch of Hybrid Buttercream per the recipe instructions. Transfer 1 cup of the buttercream to a piping bag fitted with piping tip 4B. Secure the bag with a clip.

4. Divide the remaining buttercream into two equal-size batches. Color one batch orange brown (mixing orange and brown food colorings) and then transfer to a piping bag fitted with piping tip 1A. Color the second batch golden brown (mixing brown and yellow food colorings) and then transfer to a piping bag fitted with piping tip 18. Secure the bags with clips.

Decorating

1. Use the orange buttercream to pipe a dollop of buttercream on top of the cupcakes. Hold the piping bag upright with the tip just above the center of the cupcake. Squeeze and slowly pull upward, then release the pressure and pull away, leaving a ½-inch (1.25cm) gap around the edge to allow for spreading when the cupcakes are pressed down. *(see Photo 1)*

2. Gently press the cupcakes onto the prepared baking sheet. (Don't push down too hard; you want to be sure that there is enough space around the edges for the pie crust.) Transfer the baking sheet to the freezer for 15 to 20 minutes or until the buttercream peels away from the paper cleanly. (See "Using the Flip-and-Freeze Method" on page 18.) Remove the baking sheet from the freezer and peel the cupcakes away from the parchment paper. *(see Photo 2)*

3. Use the light brown buttercream to pipe the pie crust around the edges of the cupcakes. To create a shell-like border, hold the piping bag and squeeze while pulling away to the right to create a shell shape. Continue around the edges, overlapping the tail of each shell as you go. *(see Photo 3)*

4. Use the plain buttercream to pipe the whipped cream in the center of each cupcake. Hold the piping bag upright with the piping tip just above the orange buttercream. Squeeze the bag and gently pull away. *(see Photo 4)*

Shaped Christmas Trees

'Tis the most wonderful time to make the most wonderful Christmas tree cupcakes! Shaped like mini trees with chocolate trunks, these little cuties will be the talk of the Christmas party. You can decorate them as fancy as you like. Why not add a sprinkle of edible glitter for some extra sparkle?

Prep time

40 minutes

Baking time

20 minutes

Decorating time

40 minutes

Makes

12 cupcakes

EQUIPMENT

12-cup cupcake pan

12 foil cupcake liners

1 piping bag

1 small round piping tip (12)

48 foil squares

Rolling pin

Small star-shaped cutter

Tweezers

INGREDIENTS

12 Chocolate Cupcakes (p. 25)

1 batch Basic Buttercream (p. 33)

Green food coloring

1 (50g [1.75oz]) piece yellow fondant

Colored sprinkle balls

6 Reese's Miniature Cups, each cut in half

Gold luster dust

Edible glitter (optional)

Prep and Baking

1. Make the cupcake batter per the recipe instructions. Line a 12-cup cupcake pan with foil liners.

2. Fold half the foil squares into rectangles and then tightly roll the other half into balls.

3. Fill the liners half full with cupcake batter. Insert two foil squares near the top end of the cupcake to create the top of the tree. Pinch the liner into a point at the top. *(see Photo 1)*

4. Add two foil balls at the bottom of the cupcake to create the shape of the trunk. Bake as instructed and allow to cool completely before decorating. *(see Photo 2)*

5. Make a batch of Basic Buttercream per the recipe instructions. Color it green and transfer it to a piping bag fitted with a round piping tip 12. Secure the bag with a clip.

6. Use a rolling pin to roll out a piece of yellow fondant to approximately 2mm thickness. Use a small star cutter to cut out 12 stars. Brush them with gold luster dust. *(see Photo 3)*

1

2

3

Decorating

1. Holding the cupcake with the pointed part (top) facing you, use the green buttercream to pipe four dots across the top of the cupcake, leaving the trunk space as it is for now. *(see Photo 4)*

4

2. Use the largest end of a small piping tip to spread the dots downward. Repeat with a row of three dots and then a row of two dots, and finish at the point with one dot. *(see Photo 5)*

3. Use tweezers to add some round sprinkles to replicate baubles. Add a fondant star to the top of the tree. *(see Photo 6)*

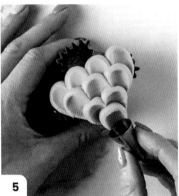

5

4. Apply a small amount of buttercream to the trunk part of the cupcake and place the half Reese's Miniature Cup on top to create the trunk. Sprinkle the edible glitter over the top (if using). *(see Photo 7)*

6

7

Snow-Covered Christmas Trees

It's beginning to look a lot like Christmas! Treat your friends and family over the festive season with these unique Christmas tree cupcakes. They are so much fun to decorate and really easy to make. They're decorated with sugar pearls for baubles and a dusting of powdered sugar for snow—your guests will be left dreaming of a white Christmas!

Prep time
40 minutes

Baking time
20 minutes

Decorating time
30 minutes

Makes
12 cupcakes

EQUIPMENT

12-cup cupcake pan

12 foil cupcake liners

2 piping bags

1 large open star piping tip (8B)

1 large open star piping tip (4B)

Rolling pin

Small star-shaped cutter

Palette knife

Tweezers

Baking sheet

Parchment paper

Fine-mesh sieve

INGREDIENTS

12 Cookie Dough Cupcakes (p. 32)

1 batch Basic Buttercream (p. 33)

Green food coloring

White sanding sugar or desiccated coconut

12 chocolate Pocky Sticks

Colored sprinkle balls

1 (50g [1.75oz]) piece yellow fondant

Confectioners' sugar

1   2   3

Prep and Baking

1. Make the cupcake batter per the recipe instructions. Line a 12-cup cupcake pan with foil cupcake liners and then fill the liners two-thirds full with batter. Bake as instructed and allow to cool completely before decorating.

2. Make a batch of Basic Buttercream per the recipe instructions. Transfer one-third of the buttercream to a separate bowl, cover the bowl, and set it aside. Color the remaining buttercream green and transfer half to a bag fitted with piping tip 8B and the other half to a bag fitted with piping tip 4B. Secure the bags with clips.

3. Use a rolling pin to roll out a piece of yellow fondant to approximately 2mm thickness. Use a small star cutter to cut out 12 stars.

Decorating

1. Use a palette knife to spread a layer of the white buttercream over the top of the cupcakes. (It doesn't need to be a thick layer; it just needs to be just enough to cover the surface to create a snowy effect.) Sprinkle the cupcakes lightly with the sanding sugar or desiccated coconut. *(see Photo 1)*

4   5   6

2. To ensure all the trees are the same height, take one of the Pocky Sticks and push it into the center of a cupcake. Decide how tall you would like the trees to be and then break off the rest of the stick. Take the stick out and cut the remaining Pocky Sticks to the same size. Push a Pocky Stick straight down into the center of each cupcake. *(see Photo 2)*

3. Use the green buttercream to pipe the bottom part of the tree. Hold the piping bag upright over the Pocky Stick and push the bag down onto the stick until the piping tip nearly touches the cupcake. Gently squeeze the bag until you have the right size for the bottom of the tree, then lift the bag a little and squeeze again. Continue squeezing and lifting, making each layer slightly smaller than the previous layer, until you are halfway up the Pocky Stick, then switch to piping tip 4B to complete the top part of the tree. *(see Photo 3)*

4. Decorate the trees using the different-size sprinkle balls. (I like to use tweezers for this part as I like them to look neat and tidy. However, you can always sprinkle them over the top.) *(see Photo 4)*

5. Add a fondant star to the top of each tree. *(see Photo 5)*

6. To create the snow effect, set the cupcakes on a parchment-lined baking sheet. Sprinkle small amounts of confectioners' sugar through a fine-mesh sieve and over the tops of the trees. *(see Photo 6)*

Frosty and Friends (Snowmen)

Don't melt the snowman . . . eat him, instead! These simple snowman cupcakes are a must for any Christmas party, winter birthday party, or just for a fun baking activity with the kids. You could use sour straps for his scarf if you don't have the piping tip listed. If you are not a fan of coconut, swap it for finely grated white chocolate. Yum!

Prep time
40 minutes

Baking time
20 minutes

Decorating time
30 minutes

Makes
12 cupcakes

EQUIPMENT

12-cup cupcake pan

12 foil cupcake liners

3 piping bags

1 large round piping tip (1A)

2 small basket weave piping tips (48)

24 foil balls

Tweezers

Toothpick

INGREDIENTS

12 Chocolate Cupcakes (p. 25)

1 batch Bright White Buttercream (p. 33)

Food coloring (red, blue)

Desiccated coconut

24 black round sprinkles

12 orange long sprinkles

24 colored sprinkles

Mini black round sprinkles

1   2   3

Prep and Baking

1. Make the cupcake batter per the recipe instructions. Line a 12-cup cupcake pan with foil cupcake liners and then fill the liners half full with batter. Insert a foil ball into both sides of the liner, just above halfway so the top half is slightly smaller than the bottom. Bake as instructed and then allow to cool completely before decorating. *(see Photo 1)*

2. Make a batch of Bright White Buttercream per the recipe instructions. Divide the batch in half. Keep one half white and then divide the other half into two equal-size portions. Color one portion red and one portion blue. Transfer to two separate piping bags, each fitted with piping tip 48. Secure the bags with clips.

Decorating

1. Using a medium round piping tip 1A, pipe the shape of the snowmen with the white buttercream. For the head, pipe a large dot of buttercream in the center of the top part of the cupcake, leaving a ¼-inch (0.5cm) gap around the edges. (The dot will spread when it is pushed into the coconut.) For the body, pipe a circle of buttercream in the center of the bottom part of the cupcake. Start at the top and pipe a swirl, finishing in the middle, again leaving a ¼-inch (0.5cm) gap around the edges. *(see Photo 2)*

2. Pour the desiccated coconut into a bowl. Press the buttercream into the coconut as gently as possible, trying to keep the shape of the snowman as perfect as you can. *(see Photo 3)*

3. Use tweezers to add two black round sprinkles for the eyes and an orange sprinkle for the nose. *(see Photo 4)*

4. Use a toothpick to poke holes for the smile and then use the tweezers to add a mini black sprinkle to each hole. *(see photo 5)*

5. Use the red buttercream to pipe the scarves onto six of the cupcakes. Hold the piping bag at the top of the snowman's body and pipe a slightly curved line from left to right. Pipe another line downward, pulling out to the right for the second part of the scarf. Repeat this step with the blue buttercream for the remaining six cupcakes. *(see Photo 6)*

6. Use tweezers to add two colored sprinkles for the buttons. *(see Photo 7)*

Frosty and Friends (Snowmen) 99

Santas

Ho, ho, ho! Santa Claus is coming to town! Are you looking for a treat to leave out for Santa this year? I've got your back. Get the kiddies involved in decorating a batch of these jolly, cute Santa cupcakes. Don't forget to leave one out for Rudolph, too; he might not want his carrot this year!

Prep time

1 hour

Baking time

20 minutes

Decorating time

40 minutes

Makes

12 cupcakes

EQUIPMENT

12-cup cupcake pan

12 cupcake liners

3 piping bags

1 small open star piping tip (18)

1 jumbo round piping tip (809)

1 large round piping tip (2A)

Baking sheet

Parchment paper

Tweezers

INGREDIENTS

12 Chai Latte Cupcakes (p. 31)

1 batch Bright White Buttercream (p. 33)

Food coloring (red, pink)

24 black round sprinkles

12 red M&M's

1 **2** **3**

Prep and Baking

1. Line a baking sheet with parchment paper. Set aside.

2. Make the cupcake batter per the recipe instructions. Line a 12-cup cupcake pan with cupcake liners and then fill the liners three-quarters full with batter. Bake as instructed and allow to cool completely before decorating.

3. Make a batch of Bright White Buttercream per the recipe instructions and divide the buttercream into three equal-size portions. Leave one portion white and transfer it to a piping bag fitted with piping tip 18; color one portion with a small amount of pink food coloring and transfer it to a piping bag fitted with piping tip 809; color the last portion red and transfer it to a piping bag fitted with piping tip 2A. Secure the bags with clips and set aside.

Decorating

1. Use the pink buttercream to pipe a dollop on top of each cupcake. Hold the piping bag upright and just above the center of the cupcake, squeeze and slowly pull upward, then release the pressure and pull away, leaving a ¼-inch (0.5cm) gap around the edge to allow for spreading when the cupcakes are pressed down. *(see Photo 1)*

4

5

6

2. Press the cupcakes down on the prepared baking sheet. (See "Using the Flip-and-Freeze Method" on page 18.) Transfer the baking sheet to the freezer for 15 to 20 minutes to allow the buttercream to set and then remove the baking sheet from the freezer and peel the cupcakes from the parchment paper.

3. Use the red buttercream to pipe the hats. Hold the piping bag at an angle, then start at one side of the cupcake and pipe a line across to the other side and then back again, getting smaller each time. Continue until you reach the top and then pull away to one side. *(see Photo 2)*

4. Use the white buttercream to add a pom-pom and fur around the edges of the hat. Hold the piping bag upright, squeeze out a star shape and then pull away. Continue across the bottom of the hat. *(see Photo 3)*

5. For the beard, use the white buttercream to pipe a line of stars around the bottom edge of the cupcake and then add another line of stars just above the previous line and from one side of the hat fur to the other. *(see Photo 4)*

6. Add a moustache using the white buttercream. Starting in the center of the beard, pipe two curved lines, one going each way. *(see Photo 5)*

7. Push a red M&M over the center of the moustache for a nose. Use tweezers to add two black round sprinkles for the eyes. *(see Photo 6)*

chapter 4

Special OCCASIONS

Wedding Day 107

Happy Birthday!. 111

Birthday Magic! 115

High Heels (Bridal Showers). 119

Graduation Caps 122

It's a Baby! (Baby Showers or
  Gender Reveals). 125

Mother's Day Flower Power
  (Daisies and Sunflowers) 131

Wedding Day

Celebrate your big day with beautiful wedding cupcakes. These gorgeous, yet surprisingly simple flowers will add a touch of elegance to your special occasion. You can make these any color; you can even match them to your bouquet. They would also be perfect for Mother's Day, engagement parties, or just for a flower-loving friend.

Prep time
40 minutes

Baking time
20 minutes

Decorating time
1 hour

Makes
12 cupcakes

EQUIPMENT

12-cup cupcake pan

24 cupcake liners

1 piping bag

1 large open star piping tip (1M)

Baking sheet

Parchment paper

Small spoon

INGREDIENTS

12 Lemon Cupcakes (p. 29)

1 batch Bright White Buttercream (p. 33)

340g (12oz) white candy melts

1 package silver sugar pearls

1

2

3

Prep and Baking

1. Line a baking sheet with parchment paper. Set aside.

2. Make the cupcake batter per the recipe instructions. Line a 12-cup cupcake pan with cupcake liners and then fill the liners two-thirds full with the batter. Bake as instructed and allow to cool completely before decorating.

3. Make a batch of Bright White Buttercream per the recipe instructions. Transfer the buttercream to a piping bag fitted with piping tip 1M. Secure the bag with a clip.

Decorating

1. To make the flowers, melt the white candy melts in a microwave-safe bowl. (See "Working with Candy Melts" on page 21.) Dip the back of a small spoon into the candy melts, coating the tip with a layer of the melted candy. *(see Photo 1)*

2. Hold the spoon over the parchment paper and spread the candy onto the parchment paper to create petal shapes. (Each flower will have 10 petals.) Transfer the baking sheet to the fridge for 15 minutes to allow the petals to set. (Note that you will need to wipe the spoon clean as the candy begins to harden. You can keep the bowl of candy melts workable by reheating it as needed.) *(see Photo 2)*

3. Line a 12-cup cupcake pan with the remaining liners to assemble the flowers in. Add a blob of the melted candy to the bottom of a cupcake liner. Add six petals to the liners, one at a time, sitting the small ends of the petals into the melted candy and letting the large ends rest on the cupcake liner. Each petal should be slightly overlapping the next, and the petals should complete a circle in the liner. (You can use a toothpick to make it easier to move the petals.) *(see Photo 3)*

4

4. Add a smaller amount of melted candy to the middle of the liner, and arrange four more petals in the center of the flower. (If needed, you can place small foil balls against these interior petals to keep them in place, just be sure to remove them just as the candy begins to set and before the candy sets completely.) *(see Photo 4)*

5

5. Add silver sugar pearls to the center of each flower. *(see Photo 5)*

6. Transfer the cupcake pan to the fridge for 15 minutes to allow the flowers to set. Leave them in the liners until you are ready to add them to the cupcakes.

7. Use the white buttercream to pipe a swirl onto each cupcake. Hold the piping bag upright and just above the center of the cupcake. Squeeze out a dot of buttercream and then move the tip in a circle around the dot. Continue squeezing the bag while moving up in a spiral until you reach the desired height. End the spiral at the center of the cupcake by stopping the squeezing before pulling the tip away. *(see Photo 6)*

6

8. Carefully remove the flowers from the cupcake liners and set them on top of the buttercream swirls. Push them down very gently until they are secured. *(see Photo 7)*

7

Happy Birthday!

You can have your cake and eat it, too, with these colorful birthday cupcakes. A Reese's Miniature Cup makes the perfect mini cupcake to sit on top of a delicious swirl of rainbow buttercream. Add some candles and celebrate that big day the right way. Such a fun birthday cake alternative!

Prep time
1 hour

Baking time
20 minutes

Decorating time
30 minutes

Makes
12 cupcakes

EQUIPMENT

12-cup cupcake pan

12 cupcake liners

2 piping bags

1 large open star piping tip (1M)

1 small open star piping tip (21)

Cling film

12 skinny candles

INGREDIENTS

12 Rainbow Cupcakes (p. 30)

1 batch Basic Buttercream (p. 33)

Food coloring (red, orange, yellow, green, blue, purple)

12 Reese's Miniature Cups

Colored sprinkles

 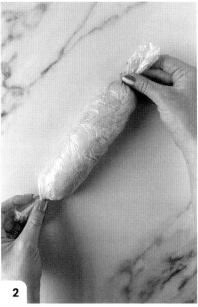 

Prep and Baking

1. Make the cupcake batter per the recipe instructions. Line a 12-cup cupcake pan with cupcake liners. Fill the liners three-quarters full with batter. Bake as instructed and allow to cool completely before decorating.

2. Make a batch of Basic Buttercream per the recipe instructions. Divide the buttercream into six equal-size portions. Color one portion red, one portion orange, one portion yellow, one portion green, one portion blue, and one portion purple.

3. Place a long piece of cling film (approximately 20 inches [50cm]) onto a flat surface. Use a rubber spatula to scoop out the first color of buttercream and spread it out in a long line onto one end of the cling film. (See "Piping a Multicolored Swirl" on page 19.) Repeat this step with the remaining colors, lining them up next to each other. *(see Photo 1)*

4. Gently roll the cling film into a sausage shape. Lift one edge of the cling film and pull it over until the buttercream is cylindrical, tuck the edges in, and continue rolling it into a sausage shape. Twist both ends of the cling film to secure the buttercream. Set aside. *(see Photo 2)*

5. Fit the piping bag with piping tip 1M, cut off one end of the buttercream sausage, and add it to the piping bag.

4   5   6

Decorating

1. Use the rainbow buttercream to add a swirl onto each cupcake. Hold the piping bag upright and just above the center of the cupcake. Squeeze out a dot of buttercream and then move the tip in a circle around the dot. Continue squeezing the bag while moving up in a spiral until you reach the desired height, then stop squeezing and pull the tip away, ending the spiral in the center of the cupcake. *(see Photo 3)*

2. Transfer the buttercream sausage to a piping bag fitted with piping tip 21. Pipe a mini swirl on top of each Reese's Miniature Cup. (Follow the previous step for how to pipe the swirl.) Add some colored sprinkles to the swirl. *(see Photo 4)*

3. Insert a candle into the center of each mini buttercream swirl. (If needed, use a sharp knife to cut the candles to a smaller size.) *(see Photo 5)*

4. Carefully set the mini cupcake on top of the large cupcake swirl. *(see Photo 6)*

Birthday Magic!

These gravity-defying cupcakes definitely have the "wow" factor. They're the perfect way to impress your guests at a birthday party or celebration, and they're surprisingly simple to create. Once you know how to decorate them, you can use your imagination to create different variations.

Prep time

40 minutes

Baking time

20 minutes

Decorating time

40 minutes

Makes

12 cupcakes

EQUIPMENT

12-cup cupcake pan

12 cupcake liners

1 piping bag

1 large open star piping tip (8B)

Scissors

Silicone spatula

Tweezers

INGREDIENTS

12 Chocolate Cupcakes (p. 25)

1 batch Chocolate Buttercream (p. 34)

250g (8.75oz) M&M's Minis

12 M&M's Fun Size packets

100g (3.5oz) dark chocolate

13 chocolate Pocky Sticks

Prep and Baking

1. Line a baking tray with parchment paper. Set aside.

2. Make the cupcake batter per the recipe instructions. Line a 12-cup cupcake pan with cupcake liners and then fill the liners three-quarters full with batter. Bake as instructed and then allow to cool completely before decorating.

3. Make a batch of Chocolate Buttercream per the recipe instructions. Transfer the buttercream to a piping bag fitted with piping tip 8B. Secure the bag with a clip.

Decorating

1. Using scissors, carefully cut one corner from each of the M&M's Fun Size packages. (The hole should be just large enough to remove the candies.) Pour the regular M&M's into a container and keep them for something else. Set the empty wrappers aside. Pour the M&M's Minis onto the prepared baking tray. *(see Photo 1)*

2. Add the dark chocolate to a microwave-safe bowl and heat until mostly melted. Remove from the microwave and stir until smooth.

3. Use a silicone spatula to coat the top 3 inches (7.5cm) of a Pocky Stick with the melted dark chocolate. *(see Photo 2)*

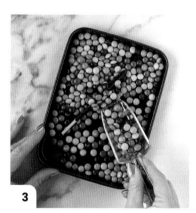

4. Set the Pocky Stick on top of the M&M's Minis and scoop extra from the sides onto the top of the stick. When the stick is completely covered, leave it until the chocolate has set. Once the chocolate is set, lift the stick from the tray. The candy will be stuck in position. To fill in any gaps, dip the end of an M&M into the melted chocolate and stick it in place. Repeat for 12 Pocky Sticks. Set aside. *(see Photo 3)*

5. Use the chocolate buttercream to pipe a large dollop onto the top of each cupcake. Hold the piping bag upright and just above the center of the cupcake. Squeeze the bag until you have the correct amount of buttercream, then lift, release the pressure, and pull away. *(see Photo 4)*

5

6. Use a spare Pocky Stick to make holes in the centers of the cupcakes. Carefully push the decorated Pocky Sticks into the holes. (You may need to trim the decorated sticks to size first.) *(see Photo 5)*

7. Use tweezers to add additional M&M's Minis to the buttercream, starting at the bottom of the stick and working down one side of the cupcake. *(see Photo 6)*

8. Add a small amount of melted chocolate to the insides of the M&M's wrappers, and place the wrappers over top of the Pocky Sticks. (The chocolate will secure the wrappers in place.) *(see Photo 7)*

6

7

High Heels (Bridal Showers)

Get the girls together to make these fabulously fun high-heel cupcakes. This design can be made in any color to suit the style of the celebration. Add all sorts of decorations to jazz them up however you like. They're perfect for a bridal shower, a girl's night, or even Mother's Day. This is also a fun kid's activity for a princess-themed party.

Prep time
40 minutes

Baking time
20 minutes

Decorating time
40 minutes

Makes
12 cupcakes

EQUIPMENT

12-cup cupcake pan

12 silver or white cupcake liners

2 piping bags

1 large open star piping tip (1M)

1 small open star piping tip (18)

Small serrated knife

Baking sheet or serving board

Tweezers

INGREDIENTS

12 Chocolate Chip Cupcakes (p. 24)

1 batch Bright White Buttercream (p. 33)

12 rolled wafer cookies (Pirouline or Pepperidge Farm brands work well)

12 Pepperidge Farm Milano cookies

50g (1.75oz) white candy melts

Silver and white sugar pearls

Prep and Baking

1. Make the cupcake batter per the recipe instructions. Line a 12-cup cupcake pan with cupcake liners and then fill the liners three-quarters full with batter. Bake as instructed and allow to cool completely before decorating.

2. Make a batch of Bright White Buttercream per the recipe instructions. Transfer approximately 1 cup of the buttercream to a piping bag fitted with piping tip 18. Add the remaining buttercream to a piping bag fitted with piping tip 1M. Secure the bags with clips.

Decorating

1. Pipe a swirl on top of each cupcake. Hold the piping bag with piping tip 1M upright at the edge of the cupcake, then squeeze out the buttercream while moving the tip in a swirling motion around the edge of the cupcake, finishing the swirl in the center. *(see Photo 1)*

2. Use a small serrated knife to trim the wafer sticks to create the heels. Cut the end that will attach to the Milano cookie at a slight angle. Each heel should be approximately 3 inches (8cm) in height. *(see Photo 2)*

3. Melt the white candy melts in a microwave-safe bowl. (See "Working with Candy Melts" on page 21.)

4. To assemble the shoes, it's best to put them together on the board or baking sheet that you will be serving them on, as they are quite fragile when they are made. (Have all your ingredients together in one place before you get started on this step.) Add a small amount of buttercream to the baking sheet or board to anchor the cupcake into position. Place the cupcake onto the baking sheet or serving board. *(see Photo 3)*

5. Push one end of a Milano cookie into one side of the buttercream. With one hand, hold the cookie in place. With the other hand, dip the cut end of the wafer cookie into the melted candy melts and then place it under the Milano cookie to support it. Leave this for 30 minutes to allow the candy to set. *(see Photo 4)*

6. When the candy has set, use the white buttercream and piping tip 18 to pipe a shell border around the edge of the Milano cookie. Hold the piping bag and squeeze while pulling away in the same direction as the edge of the cookie to create a shell shape. Continue around the edges, overlapping the tail of each shell as you go and finishing at the opposite side of the cookie. *(see Photo 5)*

7. To decorate the shoes, use tweezers to add the white and silver sugar pearls to the buttercream swirl. *(see Photo 6)*

4

5

6

Prep time
40 minutes

Baking time
20 minutes

Decorating time
30 minutes

Makes
12 cupcakes

Graduation Caps

Congratulations! The big day is finally here, and there's no better way to celebrate than with these creative graduation cap cupcakes. These fun-and-easy treats will appeal to graduates of all ages— from kindergarten to college. For a more personal touch, swap the colors of the buttercream to match the colors of the school.

EQUIPMENT

12-cup cupcake pan

12 cupcake liners

2 piping bags

1 large open star piping tip (1M)

INGREDIENTS

12 Red Velvet Cupcakes (p. 26)

1 batch Basic Buttercream (p. 33)

Red food coloring

50g (1.75oz) milk chocolate

12 Reese's Miniature Cups

12 individually wrapped milk chocolate squares (Lindt or Ghirardelli)

24 (2-inch [5cm]) strawberry laces

12 red M&M's Minis

Prep and Baking

1. Make the cupcake batter per the recipe instructions. Line a 12-cup cupcake pan with cupcake liners and then fill the liners three-quarters full with batter. Bake as instructed and allow to cool completely before decorating.

2. Make a batch of Basic Buttercream per the recipe instructions. Color half of the batch red and keep the other half white. Add the two colors to a piping bag fitted with piping tip 1M. (See "Piping a Multicolored Swirl" on page 19.)

Decorating

1. Add a swirl of buttercream onto each cupcake. Hold the piping bag upright and just above the center of the cupcake. Squeeze out a dot of buttercream and then move the tip in a circle around the dot. Continue squeezing the bag while moving up in a spiral motion until you reach the desired height. End the spiral at the center of the cupcake. Stop squeezing before pulling the tip away. (see Photo 1)

2. To make the caps, unwrap the peanut butter cups and set them upside down on a plate. Melt the milk chocolate in a microwave-safe bowl and transfer it to a piping bag. Cut a small hole from the end of the piping bag. Pipe a small amount of melted chocolate onto the top of each Reese's Miniature Cup and place a chocolate square on top of the cup. (see Photo 2)

3. Pipe a small amount of chocolate in the middle of the square and then add the ends of two laces. Let them set in place. (see Photo 3)

4. Add another small amount of chocolate on top of the laces and stick a red M&M in place. Allow the chocolate hats to set completely before transferring them to the center of the swirl on each cupcake. (see Photo 4)

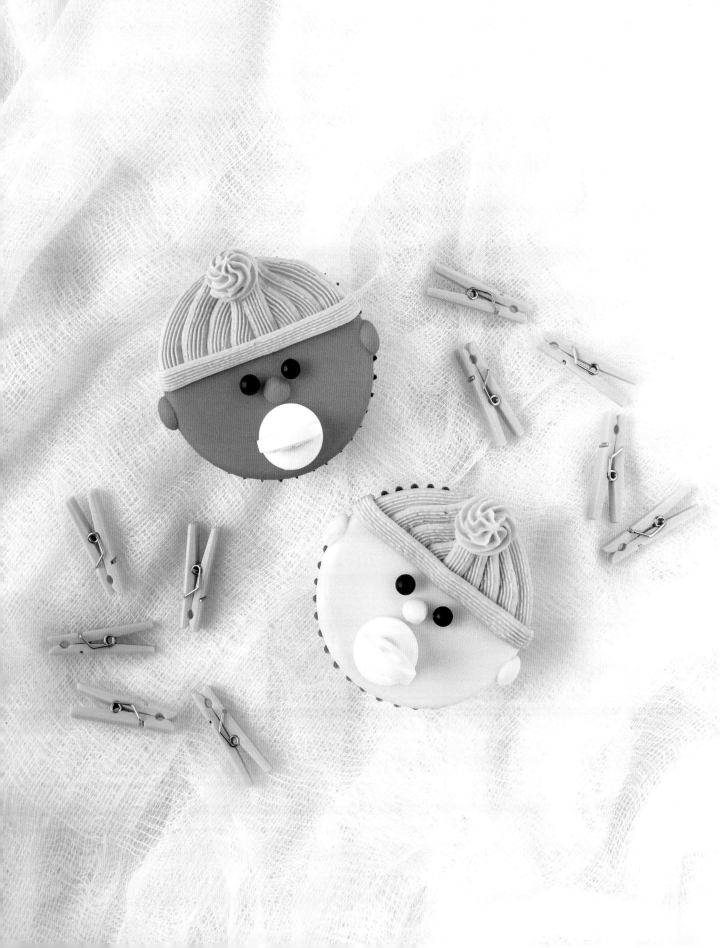

It's a Baby!
(Baby Showers or Gender Reveals)

These cupcakes can be used for a gender reveal or a baby shower. (You can skip the step for filling the cupcakes if you don't want the gender reveal.) You could also add yellow hats and a yellow jellybean to the pacifiers if you are having a gender-neutral baby shower.

Prep time
50 minutes

Baking time
20 minutes

Decorating time
40 minutes

Makes
12 cupcakes

EQUIPMENT

12-cup cupcake pan

12 cupcake liners

5 piping bags

1 jumbo round piping tip (809)

2 small basket weave piping tips (46)

1 small open star piping tip (18)

1 small round piping tip (10)

Baking sheet

Parchment paper

Small bowl filled with uncooked rice

Large straw

INGREDIENTS

12 Vanilla Cupcakes (p. 24)

1 batch Basic Buttercream (p. 33)

Food coloring (blue, brown, pink)

24 black round sprinkles

20g (0.75oz) white candy melts

24 white Life Savers candies

12 pink or blue jelly beans

Prep and Baking

1. Line a baking sheet with parchment paper. Set aside.

2. Make the cupcake batter per the recipe instructions. Line a 12-cup cupcake pan with cupcake liners and then fill the liners two-thirds full with batter. Bake as instructed and allow to cool completely before decorating.

3. Make a batch of Basic Buttercream per the recipe instructions. Divide the buttercream into three equal-size portions. For gender-reveal cupcakes, color one portion pink and one portion blue. Add the color of the gender (pink or blue) to a piping bag with no piping tip. Secure the bag with a clip and set aside. Add the other color to a piping bag fitted with piping tip 46 and secure the bag with a clip.

4. Using the orange and/or brown food coloring, color the third portion to match the desired skin tone and then add it to a piping bag fitted with piping tip 809. Secure the bag with a clip.

Decorating

1. Use the large end of a piping tip or an apple corer to remove the center of each cupcake. (Discard the cored pieces.) *(see Photo 1)*

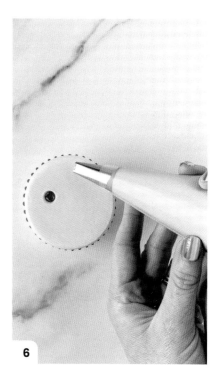

4   **5**   **6**

2. Cut the end off the piping bag containing the gender color. Fill each hole with the colored buttercream, then add the remaining buttercream to a piping bag fitted with tip 46. *(see Photo 2)*

3. Pipe a dollop of the skin-colored buttercream on top of the cupcakes. Hold the piping bag upright with the tip just above the center of the cupcake, squeeze the bag, then slowly pull upward. Release the pressure and then pull away, leaving a ¼-inch (0.5cm) gap between the buttercream and the edge of the cupcake to allow for spreading when the cupcakes are pressed down. *(see Photo 3)*

4. Gently press the cupcakes face down onto the prepared baking sheet. Transfer the baking sheet to the freezer for 15 minutes or until the buttercream peels away from the paper cleanly. (See *Using the* "Flip-and-Freeze Method" on page 18.) *(see Photo 4)*

5. While the buttercream is still cold, use a large straw to make a hole for the mouth. Hold the straw in place and gently rotate it to make a hole in the buttercream. Push it down carefully until it touches the cake and then lift it out. The buttercream should lift out with the straw, leaving the perfect hole for the pacifier to sit in. If the buttercream feels too stiff to work with, let it sit at room temperature for a minute or two. *(see Photo 5)*

6. Use piping tip 46 to pipe six pink hats and six blue hats. Start at one edge of the face, two-thirds of the way up. Hold the piping bag at an angle with the flat side of the tip touching the surface of the cupcake. *(see Photo 6)*

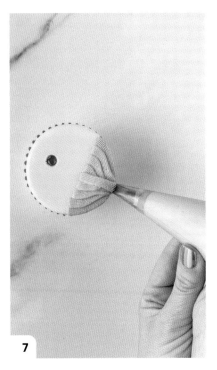 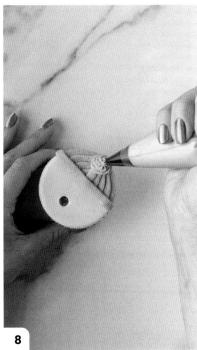 

7. Squeeze out a strip of buttercream while moving along the edge to the top and then release the pressure and pull away. Repeat this step, starting at the opposite side. Continue piping alternating lines, finishing in the center. *(see Photo 7)*

8. Pipe one long line across the bottom of the hat. Use the same color buttercream and piping tip 18 to add a swirl for the bobble on the hat. *(see Photo 8)*

9. Use tweezers to add two black round sprinkles for the eyes. Use the skin-colored buttercream and piping tip 10 to add two ears and a nose to each cupcake. Hold the piping bag at an angle with the tip touching the buttercream. Squeeze out a ball of buttercream and slowly pull away. Repeat this step for both the ears and the nose. (You can smooth them out with a palette knife if they are pointed at the ends.) *(see Photo 9)*

10. Melt the white candy melts in a separate small microwave-safe bowl. (See "Working with Candy Melts" on page 21.)

11. Lay 12 Life Savers flat on a plate. Working one at a time, dip the edges of the remaining 12 Life Savers into the melted candy and position the dipped sides onto the holes of the Life Savers that are lying flat on the plate to create pacifier handles. Transfer the plate to the fridge to allow the candy to set.

12. When the candy is set, dip one end of a jelly bean into the melted candy and insert it into the hole of the Life Saver that is not the handle. *(see Photo 10)*

13. Set the pacifiers upright in the bowl of rice and leave until the candy has set. *(see Photo 11)*

14. Insert the pacifiers into the mouths.

Mother's Day Flower Power (Daisies and Sunflowers)

Say it with cupcakes! Show Mom how much you care for her this Mother's Day with these delightful floral cupcakes. With two designs in one, she will feel spoiled! These are the perfect centerpieces for a celebration lunch, or you can box them up for a delicious and unique gift.

Prep time
40 minutes

Baking time
20 minutes

Decorating time
1 hour

Makes
12 cupcakes

EQUIPMENT

12-cup cupcake pan

12 cupcake liners

3 piping bags

1 large round piping tip (1A)

1 jumbo round piping tip (809)

1 large leaf piping tip (366)

Baking sheet

Parchment paper

Small spoon

INGREDIENTS

12 Funfetti Cupcakes (p. 24)

1 batch Basic Buttercream (p. 33)

Yellow food coloring

15g (0.5oz) cocoa powder

1 tbsp heavy cream

Yellow sanding sugar

150g (5.25oz) white candy melts

6 Oreo cookies

Prep and Baking

1. Line a baking sheet with parchment paper. Set aside.

2. Make the cupcake batter per the recipe instructions. Line a 12-cup cupcake pan with cupcake liners and then fill the liners two-thirds full with the batter. Bake as instructed and allow to cool completely before decorating.

3. Make a batch of Basic Buttercream per the recipe instructions. Transfer two-thirds of the buttercream to a medium bowl and color it yellow. Transfer half of the yellow buttercream to a bag fitted with piping tip 366 and the other half to a bag fitted with piping tip 1A. Secure the bags with clips.

4. Add the cocoa powder and heavy cream to the remaining buttercream. Mix until you have a smooth consistency. Transfer the buttercream to a piping bag fitted with piping tip 809. Secure the bag with a clip.

Decorating (Daisies)

1. Begin making the daisies by using the yellow buttercream and piping tip 1A to pipe a dollop on top of six cupcakes, leaving a ½-inch (1.25cm) gap around the edge of the cupcake. Hold the piping bag upright and just above the center of the cupcake. Squeeze the bag until you have the desired amount of buttercream and then lift and pull away. *(see Photo 1)*

2. Pour the yellow sanding sugar into a small bowl. Very gently press the buttercream into the sanding sugar so that the buttercream is covered and the dot spreads slightly, leaving a ¼-inch (0.5cm) gap around the edge of the cupcake. *(see Photo 2)*

3. Melt the white candy melts in a silicone bowl. (See "Working with Candy Melts" on page 21.)

4. Dip the back of a small spoon into the melted candy, coating the tip with a layer of candy. Hold the spoon over the parchment paper and spread the melted candy to create the petal shapes. (You will need to wipe the spoon clean each time as the chocolate will begin to harden.) Keep the bowl of candy melts workable by reheating it as needed. Transfer the baking sheet to the fridge for 15 minutes to allow the petals to set. *(see Photo 3)*

4

5. Use a sharp knife to slice off the pointed ends on each petal so they are all the same length. Carefully add them to the cupcake by pushing them at a slight angle underneath the buttercream center. *(see Photo 4)*

Decorating (Sunflowers)

1. Begin making the sunflowers by adding the Oreos to a food processor. Process until a crumb-like texture is achieved. (Alternatively, you can use a sharp knife to finely chop the Oreos.) Once crushed, transfer them to a small bowl.

5

2. Pipe a large dollop of chocolate buttercream onto the center of the remaining six cupcakes, leaving a ½-inch (1.25cm) gap around the edge of the cupcake. Hold the piping bag upright and just above the center of the cupcake. Squeeze the bag until you have the desired amount of buttercream and then lift and pull away. *(see Photo 5)*

3. Very gently press the buttercream into the Oreo crumbs, coating the buttercream and leaving a ¼-inch (0.5cm) gap around the edge of the cupcake. *(see Photo 6)*

6

4. Use the yellow buttercream and piping tip 366 to pipe a ring of buttercream petals around the chocolate center. Hold the piping bag at an angle with the point of the tip touching the cupcake. Squeeze the bag and then pull out and up slightly, releasing the pressure and pulling away sharply to create a point. (Each petal should be similar in length and width for a consistent look.) *(see Photo 7)*

7

chapter 5

Seasonal

Campfires. 137

BBQ Grills. 141

Toadstools 145

Butterflies 149

Beach Vibes. 153

Flower Pots. 157

Cactuses. 161

Pine Cones 165

Pumpkin Patch 169

Campfires

Grab the kids and gather around the kitchen to build some campfire cupcakes! This summertime dessert is perfect for a camping party over a long weekend. (Maybe give Dad a break from building the fire and treat him for Father's Day!) If you're feeling the camping vibes, toast the marshmallows before adding them to the cupcakes.

Prep time
40 minutes

Baking time
20 minutes

Decorating time
40 minutes

Makes
12 cupcakes

EQUIPMENT

12-cup cupcake pan

12 foil cupcake liners

3 piping bags

1 large round piping tip (1A)

1 small leaf piping tip (352)

1 large leaf piping tip (366)

12 toothpicks

Scissors

INGREDIENTS

12 Lemon Cupcakes (p. 29)

1 batch Basic Buttercream (p. 33)

6 Oreo cookies (finely crushed)

2 tbsp heavy cream

Food coloring (orange, red, yellow)

36 pretzel sticks

24 mini marshmallows

Prep and Baking

1. Make the cupcake batter per the recipe instructions. Line a 12-cup cupcake pan with foil cupcake liners and then fill the liners two-thirds full with the batter. Bake as instructed and allow to cool completely before decorating.

2. Make a batch of Basic Buttercream per the recipe instructions. Transfer half of the buttercream to a separate bowl and set aside. Add the crushed Oreos and heavy cream to the bowl with the remaining buttercream and then mix on low. Once the Oreos are incorporated, transfer the buttercream to a piping bag fitted with piping tip 1A. Secure the bag with a clip.

3. Divide the other half of the buttercream into three equal-size batches; color one batch red, one batch orange, and one batch yellow. Add the three colors to a sheet of cling film, roll into a sausage, then cut one end off the sausage and add it to a piping bag fitted with piping tip 366. (See "Piping a Multicolored Swirl" on page 19.)

Decorating

1. Use the Oreo buttercream to pipe the stone effect around the edges of the cupcakes. Hold the bag upright and above the cupcake, squeeze out a dot, then pull away to the right. Continue all the way around the cupcake. (The stones don't need to be exactly the same sizes. I think they look better if they are all different shapes and sizes.) *(see Photo 1)*

2. Use the multicolored buttercream to pipe the flames. Hold the piping bag upright with the piping tip just above the surface of the cupcake. Squeeze the bag, pull upward, and release. Continue piping the flames in the center of the cupcake, leaving a gap around the edge for the smaller flames. Transfer the multicolored buttercream sausage to a piping bag fitted with piping tip 352. Use this to pipe smaller flames in the gaps. *(see Photo 2)*

3. Add three pretzel sticks to each cupcake, pushing each stick through a gap between the buttercream stones and just slightly into the cupcake. Lean them into the center so that the tips of the pretzel sticks overlap in the middle. *(see Photo 3)*

4. Thread two mini marshmallows onto each toothpick. (This is easier if the toothpicks are a little damp.) For safety, use scissors to snip the sharp points off the ends of the toothpicks. Push the marshmallow sticks through a buttercream stone and slightly into each cupcake. *(see Photo 4)*

BBQ Grills

*You know summertime is in full swing when the grill is fired up!
Why not fire up the oven and get creative with these adorable grill
cupcakes? They're perfect for Father's Day, Memorial Day, the Fourth
of July, Labor Day, or just for some summertime fun. Whatever the
celebration, this showstopper cupcake will be one to remember!*

Prep time
40 minutes

Baking time
20 minutes

Decorating time
40 minutes

Makes
12 cupcakes

EQUIPMENT

12-cup cupcake pan

12 cupcake liners

4 piping bags

1 large round piping tip (1A)

1 small leaf piping tip (352)

1 large leaf piping tip (366)

Baking sheet

Parchment paper

24 toothpicks

Ruler

Scissors

INGREDIENTS

12 Peanut Butter and Jelly Cupcakes (p. 27)

1 batch Basic Buttercream (p. 33)

Food coloring (orange, red, yellow)

25g (1oz) cocoa powder

2 tbsp heavy cream

150g (5.25oz) dark cocoa candy melts

24 chocolate Pocky Sticks

48 gummy bears, each cut in half crosswise

Prep and Baking

1. Line a baking sheet with parchment paper. Set aside.

2. Make the cupcake batter per the recipe instructions. Line a 12-cup cupcake pan with cupcake liners and then fill the liners two-thirds full with the batter. Bake as instructed and allow to cool completely before decorating.

3. Make a batch of Basic Buttercream per the recipe instructions. Transfer half of the buttercream to a separate bowl and set aside. Add the cocoa powder and the heavy cream to the other half and mix until smooth. Transfer to a piping bag fitted with piping tip 1A. Secure the bag with a clip.

4. Divide the remaining half of the buttercream into three equal-size batches; color one batch red, one batch orange, and one batch yellow. Add the three colors to a piece of cling film, roll the buttercreams into a sausage, then cut off one end. Add the buttercream sausage to a piping bag fitted with piping tip 366. (See "Piping a Multicolored Swirl" on page 19.) Secure the bag with a clip.

Decorating

1. Use the chocolate buttercream to pipe the border around the edges of the cupcake. Hold the bag upright above the cupcake, squeeze out a dot, then pull away to the right, continuing all the way around the cupcake. *(see Photo 1)*

2. Use the multicolored buttercream to pipe the flames. Hold the piping bag upright with the piping tip just above the surface of the cupcake. Squeeze the bag, pull upward, then release. Continue piping the flames in the center of the cupcake, leaving a gap around the edge for the smaller flames. Transfer the buttercream sausage to a piping bag fitted with piping tip 352 and fill in the gaps by piping smaller flames. *(see Photo 2)*

1

2

3

4

3. Cut the Pocky Sticks to the size that you would like them to be and add them to the cupcake. Push each stick through the chocolate buttercream and into the cupcake. (The four sticks should create a square grid for the grill to sit on.) *(see Photo 3)*

4. Use a ruler to measure the square at the top of the Pocky Sticks. (This is to ensure the grill is the correct size to sit on top of the sticks.) Draw the measured square size onto the sheet of parchment paper to create a template. (You can draw more than one of these and work on several at a time.) Turn the sheet over so the chocolate won't be directly touching the pencil marks. *(see Photo 4)*

5

5. Melt the dark cocoa candy melts. (See "Working with Candy Melts" on page 21.) Transfer the melted chocolate to a piping bag and cut off the end of the piping bag to create a small hole. Use the template to pipe the chocolate grill tops onto the parchment paper. Add three chocolate lines across the middle of each square to create the grill tops. Let them set until firm and then go over the outlines again to ensure the grill tops are strong enough to hold the skewers. Transfer the grill tops to the fridge for 15 minutes to set. *(see Photo 5)*

6

6. When the grill tops are set, add a small amount of melted chocolate to the top of each Pocky Stick and set the grill tops on top of the Pocky Sticks. *(see Photo 6)*

7. Add four pieces of gummy bears to each toothpick. For safety, use scissors to snip the sharp ends off of the toothpicks, then place two skewers on each grill top. *(see Photo 7)*

7

Toadstools

These deliciously magical treats are perfect for any occasion such as a fairy-themed birthday party or a spring garden event. These cupcakes will take center stage! They are so easy to make and also perfect for kids to try their hand at.

Prep time

40 minutes

Baking time

20 minutes

Decorating time

40 minutes

Makes

12 cupcakes

EQUIPMENT

12-cup cupcake pan

12 foil cupcake liners

3 piping bags

1 large round piping tip (1A)

1 medium round piping tip (2A)

1 small round piping tip (12)

24 foil balls

Palette knife

Baking sheet

Parchment paper

INGREDIENTS

12 Lemon Cupcakes (p. 29)

1 batch Basic Buttercream (p. 33)

Red food coloring

1   2   3

Prep and Baking

1. Line a baking sheet with parchment paper. Set aside.

2. Make the cupcake batter per the recipe instructions. Line a 12-cup cupcake pan with foil liners and then fill the liners half full with the batter. Insert a foil ball into opposite sides of the liner to create a mushroom shape. Pinch the corners of the liners to help the cupcakes keep their shapes while baking. Bake the cupcakes as instructed and allow to cool completely before decorating. *(see Photo 1)*

3. Make a batch of Basic Buttercream per the recipe instructions. Divide the buttercream into two equal-size batches; color one batch red and leave the other batch white. Transfer the red buttercream to a piping bag fitted with piping tip 2A. Divide the white buttercream into two halves. Add one half to a piping bag fitted with piping tip 1A, then add the remaining half to a piping bag fitted with piping tip 12. Secure the bags with clips.

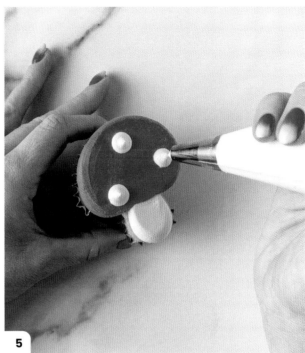

4

5

Decorating

1. Use the white buttercream and piping tip 1A to create the stem. Hold the piping bag at the bottom of the cupcake, squeeze, and pull up toward the center of the cupcake. *(see Photo 2)*

2. Use the red buttercream and piping tip 2A to pipe the top part of the toadstool. Hold the piping bag in the center of the cupcake and at the top of the stem. Pipe around the top part of the cupcake to make the shape of the toadstool, finishing in the center. (Try not to go over the edges of the liner.) Use a palette knife to smooth out the red buttercream to fill in any gaps. *(see Photo 3)*

3. Gently press the toadstools down onto the parchment paper. Transfer the baking sheet to the freezer for 15 to 20 minutes. (See "Using the Flip-and-Freeze Method" on page 18.) Remove the cupcakes from the freezer and peel them from the parchment paper. *(see Photo 4)*

4. Line the baking sheet with a clean sheet of parchment paper. Use the white buttercream and piping tip 12 to pipe four or five spots onto each cupcake. *(see Photo 5)*

5. Gently press the cupcakes onto the parchment paper and then transfer the baking sheet to the freezer for 10 minutes more. After 10 minutes, remove the cupcakes from the freezer and peel them from the parchment paper.

Butterflies

Brighten up any occasion with these stunning butterfly cupcakes! They are so easy to create, and you don't need any fancy tools to make them—just foil, a piping tip, and some sprinkles. You can use the suggested colors or change them to match the party invitations. This is a great baking project for adults and kids alike, and the cupcakes taste delicious, too.

Prep time

40 minutes

Baking time

20 minutes

Decorating time

40 minutes

Makes

12 cupcakes

EQUIPMENT

12-cup cupcake pan

12 foil cupcake liners

1 piping bag

1 large round piping tip (1A)

Small piping tip

48 foil balls

Tweezers

Small decorating brush

INGREDIENTS

12 Lemon Cupcakes (p. 29)

1 batch Hybrid Buttercream (p. 36)

Food coloring (pink, yellow)

Round black sprinkles

Long black sprinkles

Small colored sprinkles

Edible glitter (optional)

1 2 3

Prep and Baking

1. Make the cupcake batter per the recipe instructions. Line a 12-cup cupcake pan with foil liners and then fill the liners half full with batter. Insert a foil ball into both sides and the top and bottom of the liner, creating a butterfly shape. Pinch the corners of the liners to help keep their shapes while baking. Bake as instructed and allow to cool completely before decorating. *(see Photo 1)*

2. Make a batch of Hybrid Buttercream per the recipe instructions. Divide the buttercream into two equal-size portions; color one portion pink and the other portion yellow. Add the two colors to a sheet of cling film, roll into a sausage, then cut one end off the sausage and add it to a piping bag fitted with piping tip 1A. (See "Piping a Multicolored Swirl" on page 19.) Secure the bag with a clip.

Decorating

1. Starting at the top half of the cupcake, pipe a large dot at the top of each wing. *(see Photo 2)*

2. Use the largest side of a small piping tip to spread the dot downward and toward the center of the cupcake. *(see Photo 3)*

3. Pipe smaller dots a little lower down and on top of the previous ones. Use the piping tip again to spread the dots downward and toward the center of the cupcake. *(see Photo 4)*

4. Repeat this step for the bottom two wings. Make these smaller than the top wings by piping smaller dots. *(see Photo 5)*

5. Using tweezers, add a line of black round sprinkles down the center of the butterfly for the body, then add two long black sprinkles for the antennae. *(see Photo 6)*

6. Add three colored sprinkles to the top part of the large wings. Brush a small amount of the edible glitter (if using) over each butterfly. *(see Photo 7)*

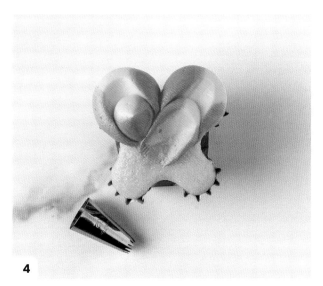

4

5

6

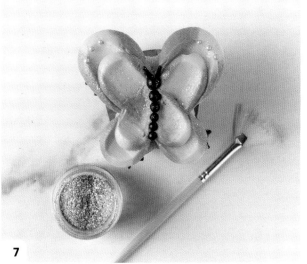

7

Beach Vibes

Are you looking for an awesome summer holiday activity? Then look no further. These beach-themed cupcakes are so much fun to decorate with the kids. Made with your favorite flavored cupcakes, buttercream waves, and cute decorations, these delightful treats are a must for birthday parties, pool parties, or just vibing at the beach.

Prep time

40 minutes

Baking time

20 minutes

Decorating time

40 minutes

Makes

12 cupcakes

EQUIPMENT

12-cup cupcake pan

12 cupcake liners

1 piping bag

1 small open star piping tip (32)

Parchment paper cut into 12 (2 × 5-inch [5 × 12.75cm]) strips

INGREDIENTS

12 Flavored Cupcakes (p. 24)

1 batch Hybrid Buttercream (p. 36)

Blue food coloring

12 shortbread cookies

3 rainbow belt candies, each cut into 4 pieces

12 Teddy Grahams

12 cocktail umbrellas

1   **2**   **3**

Prep and Baking

1. Make the cupcake batter per the recipe instructions. Line a 12-cup cupcake pan with cupcake liners and then fill the liners two-thirds full with the batter. Bake as instructed and allow to cool completely before decorating.

2. Make a batch of Hybrid Buttercream per the recipe instructions. Transfer 1 cup of the buttercream to a separate bowl, cover, and set it aside. Divide the remaining buttercream into three equal-size portions; leave one portion white, color one portion light blue, and color the third portion a darker blue. Add the three colors to a sheet of cling film, roll into a sausage, then cut one end off the sausage and add it to a piping bag fitted with piping tip 32. (See "Piping a Multicolored Swirl" on page 19.) Secure the bag with a clip.

3. Add the shortbread cookies to a food processor. Process until a fine, sand-like texture is achieved. (Alternatively, add the cookies to a ziplock plastic bag and crush them using a rolling pin.) Transfer the crushed cookies to a bowl.

Decorating

1. Put a strip of parchment paper over the top of a cupcake so that half of the cupcake is covered. *(see Photo 1)*

4   **5**   **6**

2. Use a spatula to cover the other half of the cupcake with the plain buttercream. Go over the edge of the parchment with the buttercream to create a straight line when the parchment is removed. *(see Photo 2)*

3. Gently press the buttercream into the crushed cookie mixture and then swirl it around to make sure the buttercream is completely covered. Carefully peel away the parchment paper strips. *(see Photo 3)*

4. Use the multicolored blue buttercream to pipe the waves onto the other half of the cupcake. Start at the left-hand side and next to the sand border. Hold the piping bag upright and squeeze out a dot of buttercream while moving the piping bag to the right, then release the pressure and pull away. Continue piping to the opposite side, overlapping the tail of each wave as you go. Repeat this step for two more lines of waves, with each line being smaller than the previous one. *(see Photo 4)*

5. Add a small amount of buttercream to one side of a rainbow belt candy piece and then stick it to the sand. Attach a Teddy Graham on top, again using a small amount of buttercream to ensure it stays in place. *(see Photo 5)*

6. Add the cocktail umbrella by pushing the stick into the sand behind the Teddy Graham. *(see Photo 6)*

Flower Pots

Planting flowers is so much fun, and it's even more fun when you get to eat them! If you are looking for a unique, beautiful, and impressive dessert, these flower-pot cupcakes are definitely for you. A sugar cone filled with chocolate buttercream, Oreo soil, and a chocolate flower, all on top of a delicious cupcake—what's not to love?

Prep time
40 minutes

Baking time
20 minutes

Decorating time
1 hour

Makes
12 cupcakes

EQUIPMENT

12-cup cupcake pan

12 cupcake liners

3 piping bags

1 grass piping tip (233)

1 large round piping tip (2A)

Baking sheet

Parchment paper

Serrated knife

Small spoon

INGREDIENTS

12 Strawberry Jam Cupcakes (p. 24)

1 batch Basic Buttercream (p. 33)

Green food coloring

15g (0.5oz) cocoa powder

1 tbsp heavy cream

12 sugar cones

10 Oreo cookies

150g (5.25oz) yellow candy melts

6 mini Oreo cookies

12 matcha green tea Pocky Sticks

Prep and Baking

1. Line a baking sheet with parchment paper. Set aside.

2. Make the cupcake batter per the recipe instructions. Line a 12-cup cupcake pan with cupcake liners and then fill the liners three-quarters full with the batter. Bake as instructed and allow to cool completely before decorating.

3. Make a batch of Basic Buttercream per the recipe instructions. Transfer half of the buttercream to a separate bowl, color it green, then add it to a piping bag fitted with piping tip 233. Secure the bag with a clip.

4. Add the cocoa powder and heavy cream to the remaining buttercream and mix until smooth. Transfer to a piping bag fitted with piping tip 2A. Secure the bag with a clip.

Decorating

1. Use the green buttercream to pipe the grass on top of the cupcakes. Starting at the edges and working your way into the center, hold the piping bag upright with the tip touching the cupcake, squeeze out some buttercream, then pull away, releasing the pressure when you have the desired length of grass. *(see Photo 1)*

2. Use a small, serrated knife to saw 1½-inch (4cm) tops off the sugar cones. (To prevent the cones from shattering, saw gently around the circumference of the cone instead of sawing straight through it.) *(see Photo 2)*

3. Place the plant pot on top of the grass. Push the bottom part into the buttercream to hold the pot in place. *(see Photo 3)*

4. Use the chocolate buttercream to fill the pot about three-quarters full, leaving a gap at the top for the soil. *(see Photo 4)*

5. Add the Oreo cookies to a food processor and process into crumbs. (Alternatively, you can put them in a ziplock plastic bag and crush them with a rolling pin. Just be sure to remove the cream centers if following this method.) Use a small spoon to add some soil on top of the chocolate buttercream. *(see Photo 5)*

6. Heat the yellow candy melts and transfer the melted candy to a piping bag. (See "Working with Candy Melts" on page 21.) Cut a small hole in the end of the bag. For each flower, pipe five dots onto the prepared baking sheet, with each dot being approximately ½ inch (1.25cm) wide. *(see Photo 6)*

7

7. Place a second sheet of parchment paper over the flower petals and push down gently on each dot with your finger. Each petal should now be 1 inch (2.5cm) wide. Transfer the petals to the fridge for 15 minutes to set, then remove them from the paper. *(see Photo 7)*

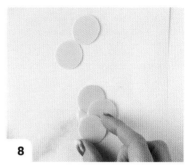

8

8. To assemble the flowers, add a small amount of melted candy onto the parchment paper. Add the petals, one at a time, with each slightly overlapping the previous petal. For the final petal, slide it into place so that one side is overlapping a petal and the other side is sitting under the first petal. *(see Photo 8)*

9

9. Separate the mini Oreo cookies into two halves and then remove and discard the cream filling. Add more melted candy to the center of each flower and carefully set an Oreo Mini half on top. Transfer the flowers to the fridge for 15 minutes to set. *(see Photo 9)*

10. Attach the Pocky Stick stem by adding some melted candy to the back of the flower. Sit the Pocky Stick in place and allow them to set for 15 minutes. *(See Photo 10)*

10

11. Add the flowers to the plant pots by pushing them through the buttercream and slightly into the cupcakes. (If needed, trim the Pocky Sticks to size with a sharp knife.) *(see Photo 11)*

11

Cactuses

These delicious cupcakes are decorated to look like miniature succulent gardens and are perfect for any party. You can get creative and make the cactuses in different colors and sizes. This "dessert from the desert" is guaranteed to be the talk of the table!

Prep time
40 minutes

Baking time
20 minutes

Decorating time
40 minutes

Makes
12 cupcakes

EQUIPMENT

12-cup cupcake pan

12 foil cupcake liners

4 piping bags

1 small open star piping tip (18)

1 large round piping tip (1A)

1 large open star piping tip (8B)

1 small leaf piping tip (352)

Tweezers

INGREDIENTS

12 Lemon Cupcakes (p. 29)

1 batch Basic Buttercream (p. 33)

Food coloring (green, pink)

24 shortbread cookies

24 chocolate Pocky Sticks

Small white sprinkles (optional)

Prep and Baking

1. Make the cupcake batter per the recipe instructions. Line a 12-cup cupcake pan with foil cupcake liners and then fill the liners two-thirds full with the cupcake batter. Bake as instructed and allow to cool completely before decorating.

2. Make a batch of Basic Buttercream per the recipe instructions. Place 1 cup of the buttercream in a bowl, color it pink, and transfer it to a piping bag fitted with piping tip 18. Secure the bag with a clip.

3. Divide the remaining buttercream into three equal-size portions. Keep one portion white and transfer it to a piping bag fitted with piping tip 1A. Divide the second portion into two smaller, equal-size portions and color one portion light green and the other portion a darker green. Add the two colors to a sheet of cling film, roll into a sausage, then cut one end off the sausage and add it to a piping bag fitted with piping tip 8B. (See "Piping a Multicolored Swirl" on page 19.) Secure the bags with clips.

4. Add the shortbread cookies to a food processor. Process until a fine, sand-like texture is achieved. (Alternatively, you can put them into a plastic ziplock bag and crush them with a rolling pin.) Transfer the crushed cookies to a bowl.

Decorating

1. Use the white buttercream to pipe a dollop on top of each cupcake, leaving a ¼-inch (0.5cm) gap around the edge. (*see Photo 1*)

2. Gently press the buttercream into the crushed cookies and swirl it around to ensure the buttercream reaches the edges of the cupcake. (*see Photo 2*)

3. Cut the Pocky Sticks to the sizes you would like the cactuses to be and then push them into the top of the cupcake, leaving enough space between them so they don't touch when you pipe the cactuses. (*see Photo 3*)

5 **6** **7**

4. Use the green buttercream to pipe the cactuses. Hold the piping bag upright over the Pocky Stick, push down onto the stick until the piping tip touches the cupcake, and squeeze the bag while gently pulling up at the same time. When you get to the top of the stick, pull the bag away and continue to the next cactus. *(see Photo 4)*

5. Pipe leaves around the bases of the cactuses. Add the buttercream sausage to a piping bag fitted with piping tip 352. Hold the bag at an angle while touching the bottom of the cactus and then squeeze and pull away. *(see Photo 5)*

6. Use the pink buttercream to pipe the small star shapes for flowers. Hold the bag upright and above the top of each cactus. Squeeze the bag and pull away. Continue until you have as many as you would like. (You can also add some around the base of the cactuses.) *(see Photo 6)*

7. Use tweezers to attach some small white sprinkles to the sides of the cactuses (if using). (This step can be quite time consuming, so you can add as many or as few as you like.) *(see photo 7)*

Pine Cones

These pine cone cupcakes are sure to become a favorite! They are the perfect dessert to make for the holidays, or a fun activity with friends or your kiddos. The chocolate cereal makes this design a piece of cake to decorate. You could also use milk chocolate buttons as an alternative if you can't get your hands on the cereal.

Prep time

40 minutes

Baking time

20 minutes

Decorating time

30 minutes

Makes

12 cupcakes

EQUIPMENT

12-cup cupcake pan

12 cupcake liners

1 piping bag

1 large round piping tip (1A)

Palette knife

Parchment paper

Fine-mesh sieve

INGREDIENTS

12 Chocolate Cupcakes (p. 25)

1 batch Chocolate Buttercream (p. 34)

20g (0.75oz) desiccated coconut

200g (7oz) Nestlé Chocapic chocolate cereal (or milk chocolate buttons)

Confectioners' sugar

1   2   3

Prep and Baking

1. Make the cupcake batter per the recipe instructions. Place the liners in the cupcake pan and then fill the liners three-quarters full with the batter. Bake as instructed and allow to cool completely before decorating.

2. Make a batch of Chocolate Buttercream per the recipe instructions. Transfer the buttercream to a piping bag fitted with piping tip 1A.

Decorating

1. Pipe a small amount of chocolate buttercream onto the cupcakes. Use a palette knife to spread it evenly until it covers the tops of the cupcakes. *(see Photo 1)*

2. Place the cupcakes onto a sheet of parchment paper and then sprinkle the desiccated coconut over the top. (Any excess coconut can be poured back into the packaging.) *(see Photo 2)*

3. Use the chocolate buttercream to pipe a stem onto the center of each cupcake. Hold the piping bag upright with the tip just above the cupcake. Squeeze out a 1-inch (2.5cm) dollop of buttercream, lift upward, then release the pressure and pull away. *(see Photo 3)*

4. Continue piping dollops on top of each other, getting smaller each time. The final height should be approximately 1½ inches (4cm). *(see Photo 4)*

5. Push the cereal pieces into the buttercream, starting at the bottom and working your way up in a spiral, pressing one cereal piece in at a time. Add each piece at an angle pointing slightly upward. *(see Photo 5)*

6. Once you've gotten to the top, add two pieces pointing straight upward. *(see Photo 6)*

7. Place all cupcakes on the parchment paper. Use a fine-mesh sieve to sprinkle a small amount of confectioners' sugar over the cupcakes to add a snow effect. *(see Photo 7)*

4

5

6

7

Pumpkin Patch

Celebrate fall with these brilliant pumpkin patch cupcakes. These delicious Chai Latte Cupcakes are sure to become an annual tradition. Serve them as a dessert centerpiece for Thanksgiving, Halloween, or a fall family get-together.

Prep time

40 minutes

Baking time

20 minutes

Decorating time

40 minutes

Makes

18 cupcakes

EQUIPMENT

12-cup cupcake pan

9 regular-size cupcake liners

12-cup mini cupcake pan

9 mini cupcake liners

3 piping bags

1 small leaf piping tip (352)

1 small round piping tip (3)

1 large open star piping tip (1M)

INGREDIENTS

18 Chai Latte Cupcakes (p. 31)

1 batch Basic Buttercream (p. 33)

Food coloring (green, orange)

12 Oreo cookies (cream centers removed)

5 chocolate Pocky Sticks, each cut into four equal-size pieces

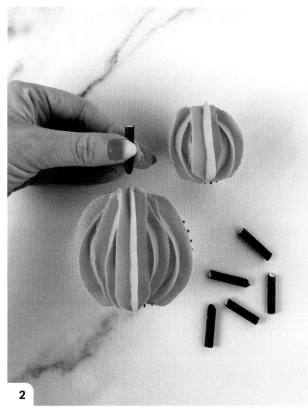

Prep and Baking

1. Make the cupcake batter per the recipe instructions. Place the liners in the cupcake pans (9 regular-size liners and 9 mini liners). Fill the liners two-thirds full with batter. Bake the mini cupcakes for 10 to 12 minutes and bake the regular-size cupcakes for 20 to 22 minutes. Allow the cupcakes to cool fully before decorating.

2. Make a batch of Basic Buttercream per the recipe instructions. Transfer 1 cup to a small bowl and color it green. Transfer half of the green buttercream to a piping bag fitted with piping tip 352 and the other half to a piping bag fitted with piping tip 3. Secure the bags with clips.

3. Color the remaining buttercream bright orange, and transfer it to a piping bag fitted with piping tip 1M. Secure the bag with a clip.

4. Use a food processor to crush the Oreo cookies. (Alternatively, you can put them into a plastic ziplock bag and crush them using a rolling pin.) Set aside.

Decorating

1. Starting with the mini cupcakes, use the orange buttercream to pipe the pumpkins. Hold the piping bag at the bottom of the cupcake and to the right of the center. Squeeze the bag and pipe a curved line of buttercream, then release the pressure and pull away at the top of the cupcake. Repeat this step on the opposite side, then pipe a line going up the middle from the bottom to the top. For the regular-size cupcakes, pipe two lines up each side and then pipe one line up the center. *(see Photo 1)*

2. Add a Pocky Stick piece to the top of each pumpkin by pushing it into the buttercream. *(see Photo 2)*

3. Use the green buttercream and piping tip 352 to add two leaves to the Pocky Stick stem. Hold the piping bag at an angle with the point of the tip touching the Pocky Stick. Squeeze the bag, pull up slightly, pause, squeeze again, then release the pressure and pull away sharply to create a point. *(see Photo 3)*

4. Use the green buttercream and piping tip 3 to add some vines. Hold the piping bag with the tip at the base of the Pocky Stick, then squeeze the bag and draw squiggly lines. Repeat this step until you have the desired amount of vines on each pumpkin. *(see Photo 4)*

5. Transfer the crushed Oreos to a serving board. Arrange the pumpkins onto the Oreo soil. If desired, pipe some additional vines across the surface of the soil.

chapter 6

Food

Melting Ice Creams 175

Hot Dogs 178

Cheeseburgers 181

Spaghetti and Meatballs 184

Fruit Pies 187

Sushi Train 191

Happy Avocados 195

Pineapples 199

Melting Ice Creams

Nothing says a hot summer quite like a melting ice cream, so why not add one to the top of a cupcake for a perfect summertime treat? Mix and match the colors and have some fun with this cute design. If you can't find mini ice cream cones, you can saw the pointed end off a regular sugar cone.

Prep time

40 minutes

Baking time

20 minutes

Decorating time

40 minutes

Makes

12 cupcakes

EQUIPMENT

12-cup cupcake pan

12 cupcake liners

3 piping bags

1 small open star piping tip (32)

1 jumbo round piping tip (809)

Baking sheet

Parchment paper

Cake pan

Saucepan

Aluminum foil

Serrated knife

INGREDIENTS

12 Cookie Dough Cupcakes (p. 32)

1 batch Basic Buttercream (p. 33)

Food coloring (pink, green)

12 mini ice cream cones (you can also cut the ends off of large cones)

100g (3.5oz) pink candy melts, chopped

30ml (1fl oz) heavy cream

Mini rainbow sprinkles

1 2 3

Prep and Baking

1. Line a baking sheet with parchment paper. Set aside.

2. Make the cupcake batter per the recipe instructions. Line a 12-cup cupcake pan with foil cupcake liners and then fill the liners two-thirds full with the batter. Bake as instructed and allow to cool completely before decorating.

3. Make a batch of Basic Buttercream per the recipe instructions. Transfer 1 cup of the buttercream to a bowl and color it pink to match the color of the candy melts. Transfer it to a piping bag fitted with piping tip 32. Color the remaining buttercream green and transfer it to a piping bag fitted with piping tip 809. Secure the bags with clips.

Decorating

1. Pipe a dollop of the green buttercream on top of the cupcakes. Hold the piping bag upright with the tip just above the center of the cupcake. Squeeze the bag and slowly pull upward, then release the pressure and pull away, leaving a ¼-inch (0.5cm) gap around the edge to allow for spreading when the cupcakes are pressed down. *(see Photo 1)*

4 **5** **6**

2. Gently press the cupcakes face down onto the prepared baking sheet. Transfer the baking sheet to the freezer for 15 to 20 minutes or until the buttercream is set. (See "Using the Flip-and-Freeze Method" on page 18.) Remove the baking sheet from the freezer and peel the cupcakes away from the parchment paper. *(see Photo 2)*

3. Make an ice cream cone holder by poking 12 holes into an aluminum foil-covered cake pan. Use the pink buttercream to pipe a swirl onto the mini cones. Place the cones into the holder until you are ready to add them to the cupcakes. *(see Photo 3)*

4. Add the chopped candy melts to a bowl. Add the heavy cream to a saucepan. Heat on medium heat just until the cream is hot, *but do not boil.* Remove the pan from the heat and then pour the heavy cream over the chopped candy melts. Let the mixture sit for a few minutes and then stir until the ganache is smooth and glossy. *(see Photo 4)*

5. Transfer the ganache to a piping bag and then cut off the end. Pipe a splatter shape on top of each cupcake. *(see Photo 5)*

6. Push an ice cream cone upside down onto the ganache. *(see Photo 6)*

7. Add some mini sprinkles over the top of the ganache.

Prep time

1 hour

Baking time

20 minutes

Decorating time

30 minutes

Makes

12 cupcakes

Hot Dogs

These hot dog cupcakes are the perfect dessert for celebrating a birthday, Father's Day, or the Fourth of July. This simple design is so much fun to make! They're a modern-day twist on the nostalgic butterfly cupcakes and are guaranteed to be a crowd-pleaser.

EQUIPMENT

12-cup cupcake pan

12 foil cupcake liners

Serrated knife

1 large open star piping tip (4B)

1 large round piping tip (1A)

2 small round piping tips (4)

4 piping bags

INGREDIENTS

12 Rainbow Cupcakes (no color added) (p. 30)

1 batch Basic Buttercream (p. 33)

Food coloring (brown, red, yellow)

Prep and Baking

1. Make the cupcake batter per the recipe instructions. Fill the cupcake liners about three-quarters full with the batter.

2. Bake the cupcakes as instructed and allow to cool completely. Once cooled, place the cupcakes in the fridge to chill for 30 minutes.

3. Make a batch of Basic Buttercream per the recipe instructions. Divide the buttercream into three equal-size portions. Keep one portion white and transfer it to a piping bag fitted with piping tip 4B. Color the second portion reddish brown and transfer it to a piping bag fitted with piping tip 1A. Divide the third batch into two smaller batches. Color one batch yellow and transfer it to a piping bag fitted with piping tip 4. Color the last portion red and transfer it to a piping bag fitted with piping tip 4. Secure the bags with clips.

4. Once the cupcakes are chilled, use a serrated knife to slice the domes off the tops. (It's easier to slice the cupcakes when they are chilled.) Cut the domes in half and set them aside. *(see Photo 1)*

Decorating

1. Use the white buttercream to pipe a swirl onto the bottom half of the cupcake. *(see Photo 2)*

2. Push the cut edges of the dome halves into the buttercream swirl just enough to secure them. (This creates the hot dog bun.) Make sure you leave enough space between the two halves to pipe the hot dog. *(see Photo 3)*

3. Use the reddish-brown buttercream to pipe the hot dog. Pipe a line from one end of the bun to the other and then over and back to where you started. *(see Photo 4)*

4. Use the red and yellow buttercreams to pipe the ketchup and mustard on top of the hot dog. *(see Photo 5)*

Cheeseburgers

Did someone say cheeseburgers for dessert? Yes, please! Bring a plate of these cute and clever burger cupcakes along to your next gathering for Father's Day, Labor Day, or a summer BBQ. With chocolate buttercream burgers and vanilla buns, these delicious treats will be a definite crowd-pleaser.

Prep time
40 minutes

Baking time
20 minutes

Decorating time
40 minutes

Makes
12 cupcakes

EQUIPMENT

12-cup cupcake pan

12 cupcake liners

5 piping bags

1 large round piping tip (2A)

1 large basketweave piping tip (2B)

1 small round piping tip (12)

1 small leaf piping tip (70)

1 small round piping tip (4)

Serrated knife

INGREDIENTS

12 Vanilla Cupcakes (p. 24)

1 batch Basic Buttercream (p. 33)

Food coloring (yellow, red, green)

25g (1oz) cocoa powder

2 tbsp heavy cream

Small white sprinkles

Prep and Baking

1. Line a baking sheet with parchment paper. Set aside.

2. Make the cupcake batter per the recipe instructions. Line a 12-cup cupcake pan with cupcake liners and then fill the liners two-thirds full with the batter. Bake as instructed and allow to cool completely before decorating.

3. Make a batch of Basic Buttercream per the recipe instructions. Transfer half of the buttercream to a separate bowl and set aside. Add the remaining half of the buttercream with the cocoa powder and heavy cream to the bowl of a stand mixer. Mix on low until you achieve a smooth consistency. Transfer the chocolate buttercream to a piping bag fitted with piping tip 2A. Secure the bag with a clip.

4. Divide the reserved buttercream into three equal-size batches. Color one batch red and transfer half of the red buttercream to a piping bag fitted with piping tip 12; transfer the other half to a piping bag fitted with piping tip 4. Color one batch yellow orange and transfer to a bag fitted with piping tip 2B. Color the remaining batch green and transfer to a piping bag fitted with piping tip 70. Secure the bags with clips.

5 6 7

Decorating

1. Remove the cupcakes from the liners and use a serrated knife to cut them in half. Put the top halves of the cupcakes on a plate and carefully sprinkle the small white sprinkles over the top. *(see Photo 1)*

2. Place the bottom halves on the prepared baking sheet. Use the chocolate buttercream to pipe the burgers. Start at the edge of the cupcake and pipe a swirl, finishing in the center. Place the tray in the fridge for 15 minutes. (I do this so that the burger will hold its shape when adding the rest of the buttercream to the top of the burger.) *(see Photo 2)*

3. Use the yellow-orange buttercream to pipe four cheese corners. With the flat side of the tip facing upward, hold the tip sideways on the edge of the burger and then squeeze and drag the buttercream into the center. Repeat this step for each corner. *(see Photo 3)*

4. Use the red buttercream with piping tip 12 to add the tomato. Pipe a curved line between each cheese corner. *(see Photo 4)*

5. Use the green buttercream to create the lettuce leaves. Hold the piping bag at an angle with the tip just above the burger. Squeeze the bag and move it up and down slightly while moving over the tomato and cheese. *(see Photo 5)*

6. Use the red buttercream with piping tip 4 to pipe the ketchup. Hold the bag directly above the cupcake and pipe squiggly lines. (The lines should go to the edges of the burger to make sure it is visible when the top of the bun is added. *(see Photo 6)*

7. Add the top halves of the cupcakes onto the burgers just before serving. (Be gentle to avoid squashing the buttercream.) *(see Photo 7)*

Prep time
30 minutes

Baking time
20 minutes

Decorating time
40 minutes

Makes
12 cupcakes

Spaghetti and Meatballs

Fool your friends and family with these spaghetti and meatball cupcakes! They look savory but taste so sweet. These delicious treats are topped with buttercream spaghetti, chocolate ganache sauce, Whopper meatballs, and white chocolate Parmesan. Even the fussiest of eaters will be wanting seconds!

EQUIPMENT

12-cup cupcake pan

12 foil cupcake liners

2 piping bags

1 grass piping tip (233)

INGREDIENTS

12 Nutella Swirl Cupcakes (p. 24)

1 batch Basic Buttercream (p. 33)

Yellow food coloring

100g (3.5oz) red candy melts, chopped

30ml (1fl oz) heavy cream

36 Hershey's Whoppers candies

20g (0.75oz) white chocolate

Prep and Baking

1. Make the cupcake batter per the recipe instructions. Line a 12-cup cupcake pan with cupcake liners and then fill the cupcake liners about two-thirds full with the batter. Bake the cupcakes as instructed and allow them to cool completely before decorating.

2. Make a batch of Basic Buttercream per the recipe instructions. Begin coloring it by adding a small amount of yellow food coloring, mixing, and then gradually adding additional food coloring (if needed) until the buttercream is a pale yellow or about the color of pasta. (Keep in mind that the color can develop more over time, so don't add too much). Transfer the buttercream to a piping bag fitted with piping tip 233.

Decorating

1. Pipe the spaghetti by holding the piping bag upright and then squeezing while moving around the cupcake in a circular motion. Continue until you have as much spaghetti as desired for each cupcake. Leave a hole in the center for the red ganache to sit in. (*see Photo 1*)

2. Add the chopped candy melts to a microwave-safe bowl. Add the heavy cream to a saucepan. Heat over medium heat just until the cream is hot, *but do not boil*. Remove the pan from the heat and pour over the chopped candy melts. Let the mixture sit for a few minutes and then stir until the ganache is smooth and glossy. (*see Photo 2*)

3. Transfer the ganache to a piping bag. Cut off the end when the ganache has cooled but is still pipable. Pipe some ganache into the hole in the spaghetti.

4. Add three Whoppers on top of the red ganache and then add a bit more ganache to the top of each whopper. (*see Photo 3*)

5. Grate the white chocolate onto a plate and then sprinkle it over the top of the cupcakes. (*see Photo 4*)

Fruit Pies

Creating these blueberry and cherry pie cupcakes is as easy as . . . pie. Whether you're making them for a bake sale, a birthday, or just to share with friends, you'll be sure to wow the crowd. Topped with M&M's and a buttercream crust, these creative cupcakes are cute as can be!

Prep time

40 minutes

Baking time

20 minutes

Decorating time

1 hour

Makes

12 cupcakes

EQUIPMENT

12-cup cupcake pan

12 foil cupcake liners

3 piping bags

1 small basket weave piping tip (46)

1 small open star piping tip (18)

1 small open star piping tip (32)

INGREDIENTS

12 Chocolate Chip Cupcakes (p. 24)

1 batch Hybrid Buttercream (p. 36)

Food coloring (blue, brown, red, yellow)

Red and blue M&M's minis

1   2   3

Prep and Baking

1. Make the cupcake batter per the recipe instructions. Line a 12-cup cupcake pan with foil cupcake liners and then fill the liners two-thirds full with the batter. Bake as instructed and allow to cool completely before decorating.

2. Make a batch of Hybrid Buttercream. Divide the buttercream into two equal-size batches. Color one batch golden brown using yellow and brown food colors, and divide it between two piping bags: one fitted with piping tip 46 and a second with piping tip 18. Secure the bags with clips.

3. Divide the remaining batch into three smaller batches; color one batch red, one batch blue, and leave the remaining batch white. Transfer the white batch to a piping bag fitted with piping tip 32. Secure the bag with a clip.

4

5

Decorating

1. Use a spatula to spread a circle of the blue buttercream on top of six of the cupcakes, leaving ¼ inch (0.5cm) around the edges. Spread a circle of the red buttercream onto the remaining six cupcakes, leaving ¼ inch (0.5cm) around the edges. *(see Photo 1)*.

2. Press the red M&M's minis into the red buttercream with the logos facing down. Repeat with the blue M&M's minis. (You can do this as uniformly or as randomly as you like.) *(see Photo 2)*

3. Using the golden brown buttercream and piping tip 46, pipe the lattice on top of the M&M's minis. Starting at one side of the cupcake, pipe a straight line across to the opposite side. Repeat three more times going in the same direction, then repeat the process in a perpendicular direction. *(see Photo 3)*

4. Using the light brown buttercream and piping tip 18, pipe the pie crust around the edges of the cupcakes. To create a shell-like border, hold the piping bag and squeeze while pulling away to the right to create a shell shape. Continue around the edges, overlapping the tail of each shell as you go. *(see Photo 4)*

5. Use the white buttercream to pipe a small swirl in the center of each pie. *(see Photo 5)*

Sushi Train

Choo choo! All aboard the sushi train! If you love sushi and cupcakes, you must try these cupcakes. They're all dressed up like a plate of sushi! You will have so much fun decorating these. Swap the coconut for white sugar strands if you prefer, and feel free to play around with the candy to customize them however you like. They're perfect for any occasion or just for a fancy treat.

Prep time
40 minutes

Baking time
20 minutes

Decorating time
1 hour

Makes
12 cupcakes

EQUIPMENT

12-cup cupcake pan

6 black cupcake liners

6 white cupcake liners

1 piping bag

1 large round piping tip (2A)

Serrated knife

Palette knife

Rolling pin

Sharp knife

INGREDIENTS

12 Vanilla Cupcakes (p. 24)

1 batch Bright White Buttercream (p. 33)

Green food coloring

100g (3.5oz) shredded coconut

Orange round sugar balls

Mini orange nonpareils

3 green candy straws, cut into 1½-inch (4cm) pieces

4 orange Haribo fruits, each sliced into three pieces

6 Swedish Fish

50g (1.75oz) black fondant

Prep and Baking

1. Make the cupcake batter per the recipe instructions. Line a 12-cup cupcake pan with the cupcake liners and then fill the liners three-quarters full with the batter. Bake as instructed and allow to cool completely before decorating.

2. Make a batch of Bright White Buttercream per the recipe instructions. Scoop out ¼ cup of the buttercream and color it a bright wasabi green. Cover and set aside.

3. Transfer the remaining buttercream to a piping bag fitted with piping tip 2A. Secure the bag with a clip.

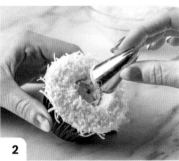

4. Use a sharp serrated knife to cut the tops off all the cupcakes so they are flush with the liners.

Decorating

1. Starting with four of the six cupcakes that have the black liners, pipe a ring of buttercream around the edges of the cupcakes. *(see Photo 1)*

2. Pour the shredded coconut into a small bowl and press the buttercream into the coconut. Swirl it around to make sure it's all covered in the coconut.

3. Use the large end of a piping tip to remake the hole in the center of the buttercream if necessary. Push it into the buttercream and move it around in a circular motion. *(see Photo 2)*

4. Add the Haribo fruits to the hole along with pieces of the green candy straws. Add some mini orange nonpareils around the buttercream to resemble tiny fish eggs. *(see Photo 3)*

5. For the two remaining cupcakes with the black liners, use a palette knife to spread a layer of buttercream onto the top of the cupcakes. Pour the orange round sugar balls into a bowl and press the buttercream into them. This will cover the top of the cupcakes to look like fish eggs. *(see Photo 4)*

6. For the six cupcakes with white liners, add a swirl of white buttercream to the top of each cupcake, leaving a ½-inch (1.25cm) gap around the edge. *(see Photo 5)*

6

7. Press the buttercream into the shredded coconut. Swirl it around in the coconut until the buttercream is covered and has spread out to the edge of the liner.

8. Add a small amount of buttercream to one side of the Swedish Fish and place them onto the tops of the cupcakes. *(see Photo 6)*

9. Use a rolling pin to roll out the black fondant as thin as possible (approximately ¹⁄₁₀ inch or 2mm). Use a sharp knife to cut it into four strips, each ½ inch (1.25cm) wide by 6 inches (16cm) long. *(see Photo 7)*

7

10. Add a small amount of buttercream to one end of the fondant strip and stick it to one side of the cupcake liner. Pull the strip over the top of the fish and down to the opposite side of the cupcake liner. Secure it in place with a small amount of buttercream. *(see Photo 8)*

11. Arrange the cupcakes on a wooden board or a serving plate. Pipe the wasabi-colored buttercream in a small serving bowl and place it with the cupcakes. *(see Photo 9)*

8

9

Happy Avocados

Holy guacamole! Could these avocado cupcakes be any cuter?! These chocolate cupcakes are filled with Nutella and then topped with buttercream and a Lindt truffle. These happy chappies are as adorable as they are delicious. They're the perfect addition to a baby shower, birthday party, or a family get-together.

Prep time
40 hour

Baking time
20 minutes

Decorating time
40 minutes

Makes
12 cupcakes

EQUIPMENT

12-cup cupcake pan

12 foil cupcake liners

3 piping bags

1 large round piping tip (2A)

1 small round piping tip (7)

Baking sheet

Parchment paper

24 foil squares

Palette knife

Tweezers

INGREDIENTS

12 Vanilla Cupcakes (colored green) (p. 24)

1 batch Basic Buttercream (p. 33)

Green food coloring

Nutella hazelnut spread

6 Lindt LINDOR milk chocolate truffles

24 black round sprinkles

24 pink round sprinkles

50g (1.75oz) black candy melts

Prep and Baking

1. Line a baking sheet with parchment paper. Set aside.

2. Make the cupcake batter per the recipe instructions.

3. Line a 12-cup cupcake pan with foil cupcake liners and then fill the liners half full with batter. Insert a foil rectangle into each side of the cupcake to create a point. Pinch the liner into a point to avoid losing the shape while baking. Bake as instructed and allow to cool completely before decorating. *(see Photo 1)*

4. Make a batch of Basic Buttercream per the recipe instructions. Scoop out 1 cup and color it dark green. Transfer it to a piping bag fitted with piping tip 7, then secure the bag with a clip. Color the remaining buttercream a lighter shade of green and then transfer it to a piping bag fitted with piping tip 2A. Secure the bag with a clip.

1

Decorating

1. Use an apple corer or a piping tip to remove a circular piece from the center of each cupcake. (Reserve the cored cake pieces.) *(see Photo 2)*

2. Add the Nutella to a microwave-safe bowl and heat just long enough that it is pourable. Add approximately 2 teaspoons of the Nutella to the center of each cupcake, then top the filling with the reserved cored cake pieces.

3. Pipe the avocado shape onto the cupcake, leaving a ¼-inch (0.5cm) gap around the edge to allow room for spreading when the buttercream is pushed down. Smooth out the buttercream with a palette knife to fill in any gaps. (Try to get the surface as smooth and flat as possible without losing the avocado shape.) *(see Photo 3)*

2

3

4

4. Use the darker green buttercream to draw an outline around the edge of the avocado shape. (For best results, stay as close to the edge as you can.) *(see Photo 4)*

5. Gently press the avocados down onto the prepared baking sheet. Transfer the baking sheet to the freezer for 15 to 20 minutes. (See "Using the Flip-and-Freeze Method" on page 18.)

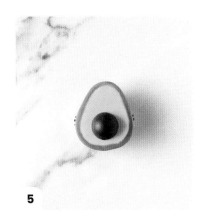

5

6. Remove the cupcakes from the freezer. Peel the cupcakes from the parchment paper. Use extra buttercream and an offset spatula to fill in any gaps, if needed.

7. Use a sharp knife to cut the Lindt truffles in half. (It's easiest to cut them down the seam. If the Lindt truffles are too soft to cut, place them in the fridge for 10 minutes before cutting.)

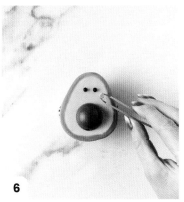

6

8. Place a Lindt half in the center of the wider portion of each cupcake. *(see Photo 5)*

9. Use tweezers to add two black round sprinkles for the eyes and two pink round sprinkles for cheeks. *(see Photo 6)*

10. Heat the black candy melts. (See "Working with Candy Melts" on page 21.) Transfer the melted candy to a piping bag fitted with piping tip 7. Secure the bag with a clip. Cut a small hole in the end of the bag and then pipe smiles onto the cupcakes. *(see Photo 7)*

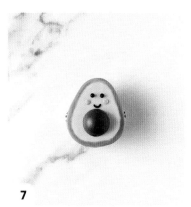

7

Pineapples

Hands up if you're feeling fruity! Brighten up any summer party with these cool and trendy pineapple cupcakes. Serve them around the pool or with a piña colada to make your next outdoor party extra special.

Prep time
40 minutes

Baking time
20 minutes

Decorating time
1 hour

Makes
12 cupcakes

EQUIPMENT

12-cup cupcake pan

12 cupcake liners

1 piping bag

1 jumbo round piping tip (809)

Baking sheet

Parchment paper

Wooden skewer

Teaspoon

INGREDIENTS

12 Flavored Cupcakes (p. 24)

1 batch Basic Buttercream (p. 33)

Yellow food coloring

Yellow sanding sugar

13 matcha green tea Pocky Sticks

150g (5.25oz) green candy melts

Prep and Baking

1. Line a baking sheet with parchment paper. Set aside.

2. Make the cupcake batter per the recipe instructions. Line a 12-cup cupcake pan with cupcake liners and then fill the liners three-quarters full with batter. Bake as instructed and allow to cool completely before decorating.

3. Make a batch of Basic Buttercream per the recipe instructions. Color the buttercream yellow and then transfer it to a piping bag fitted with piping tip 809. Secure the bag with a clip.

Decorating

1. Use the yellow buttercream to pipe a dollop of buttercream in the center of each cupcake. Hold the bag upright with the tip touching the cupcake and then squeeze, lift the bag, and pull away. *(see Photo 1)*

2. Pour the yellow sanding sugar into a small bowl. Gently press the buttercream into the sugar and swirl the cupcake around until the buttercream has spread to the edges and the sugar is covering the top evenly.

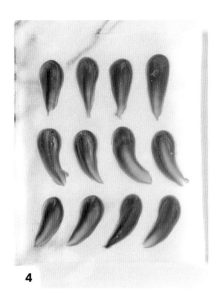

4   5   6

3. Use the wooden skewer to make indents in the buttercream. Start in the middle and lightly press the skewer down into the buttercream. Clean any excess buttercream from the skewer with a paper towel and then make the next indent. Make three indents in one direction and then three in the opposite direction, creating a diamond pattern. (If the lines lose their shape slightly, sprinkle a little extra sanding sugar into the indents and then press the skewer down into the indent again. *(see Photo 2)*

4. Melt the green candy melts in a microwave-safe bowl. (See "Working with Candy Melts" on page 21.) Dip the back of a teaspoon into the candy melts, coating the tip with a layer of melted candy. *(see Photo 3)*

5. Press the spoon onto the parchment paper and spread the candy to create leaf shapes. Wipe the spoon clean with a paper towel after each leaf. (For each pineapple, you will need one straight leaf, two curved to the right, and two curved to the left. They can be different shapes and sizes for this design.) Transfer the leaves to the fridge for 15 minutes to allow them to set. *(see Photo 4)*

6. When the leaves are set, carefully remove them from the parchment paper. Place the Pocky Sticks on the parchment paper and spoon some melted candy over the top 1 inch (2.5cm) of the sticks. Place the straight leaf onto this end, and continue adding the leaves by dipping the ends into the melted candy and affixing the leaves as desired. Transfer to the fridge for 15 minutes to allow the leaves to set. *(see Photo 5)*

7. Add the leaves to the cupcakes by using a spare Pocky Stick to make a hole in the side of each cupcake, pushing the stick into the cupcake at a slight angle. Carefully insert the stick with the leaves attached into the hole. (If needed, you can use a sharp knife to trim the ends to size.) *(see Photo 6)*

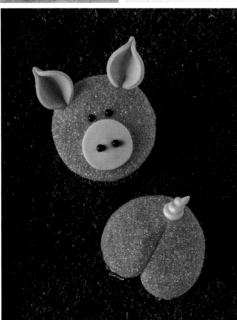

chapter 7

Animals

Turtle-y Awesome 205

Kings of the Jungle (Lions) 209

Sleepy Sloths. 213

Bunnies 217

Hip Hop Hooray! (Frogs). 221

Pigs in the Mud. 225

Penguins 228

Pupcakes 231

Turtle-y Awesome

It's turtle time! Take your cupcake game to the next level with these adorable cupcakes. These are great to make with the kids, and the gelatin shells will be a huge hit for a birthday party, baby shower, or just some summer holiday fun. They look great in any color, too.

Prep time

40 minutes

Baking time

20 minutes

Decorating time

40 minutes

Makes

12 cupcakes

EQUIPMENT

12-cup mini cupcake pan

12 mini cupcake liners

12-cup cupcake pan

12 foil cupcake liners

2 piping bags

1 large round piping tip (2A)

1 small round piping tip (12)

Metal spatula

Tweezers

INGREDIENTS

12 Funfetti Cupcakes (p. 24)

1 batch Basic Buttercream (p. 33)

4 shortbread cookies

Green food coloring

2 (85g [3oz]) packets lime gelatin

2 tbsp plain gelatin powder

235ml (8fl oz) cold water

¼ tsp edible glitter (optional)

24 mini black round sprinkles

Prep and Baking

1. Line the mini cupcake pan with the mini cupcake liners.

2. Add the shortbread cookies to a food processor. Process until a fine, sand-like consistency is achieved. Transfer to a bowl and set aside.

3. In a small microwave-safe container, combine the lime and plain gelatins along with the cold water. Whisk to combine and then leave the mixture to sit for 10 minutes. After 10 minutes, microwave the mixture for 30 seconds and then stir well. Return it to the microwave for another 30 seconds and then stir again. The gelatin should be dissolved by this stage.

4. Add the edible glitter (if using) and stir well. Pour the mixture into the mini cupcake liners and transfer the pan to the fridge for 1 hour. (Don't overfill the liners, as they can spill when you move them to the fridge. You can always top them off when they are in the fridge.)

5. Make the cupcake batter per the recipe instructions. Line a 12-cup cupcake pan with foil cupcake liners and then fill the liners two-thirds full with the batter. Bake as instructed and allow to cool completely before decorating.

6. Make a batch of Basic Buttercream per the recipe instructions. Scoop 1 cup into a bowl and cover until ready to use. Color the remaining buttercream green. Divide the green

4

5

buttercream into two equal-size batches. Add one batch of the green buttercream to a piping bag fitted with piping tip 2A and the other batch to a piping bag fitted with piping tip 12. Secure the bags with clips.

Decorating

1. Use a metal spatula to add a thin layer of the white buttercream to the tops of the cupcakes. *(see Photo 1)*

2. Press the cupcakes into the crushed-up shortbread cookies to create a sand effect. To ensure the buttercream sticks to the crumbs, make a small indent in the crumbs where you are going to pipe the head, legs, and tail. *(see Photo 2)*

3. Use the green buttercream and piping tip 2A to pipe the turtle's head. Hold the piping bag upright slightly to the left of the center of the cupcake. Squeeze the bag until you have the desired size of dot and then pull the bag inward and release the pressure. *(see Photo 3)*

4. Use the green buttercream and piping tip 12 to pipe the legs and tail. Hold the bag upright, squeeze, and pull the bag away to the right. Release the pressure and pull away to create pointy ends. Repeat this step for the tail. *(see Photo 4)*

5. Use tweezers to add two black sprinkles for the eyes. Add the gelatin shells just before serving. *(see Photo 5)*

Kings of the Jungle (Lions)

Make your party roar with these fur-ocious lion cupcakes. Bake a batch of these cute and yummy treats for a baby shower or a birthday, or just because they are so royally adorable. These are a fun activity for a rainy day with the smallies. These wild and delicious treats are sure to be the kings of any celebration!

Prep time
40 minutes

Baking time
20 minutes

Decorating time
40 minutes

Makes
12 cupcakes

EQUIPMENT

12-cup cupcake pan

12 cupcake liners

2 piping bags

1 large round piping tip (809)

1 small grass piping tip (233)

Baking sheet

Parchment paper

Small piping tip

Toothpick

Tweezers

INGREDIENTS

12 Chai Latte Cupcakes (p. 31)

1 batch Basic Buttercream (p. 33)

Food coloring (yellow, orange)

24 yellow M&M's minis

50g (1.75oz) white fondant

12 pink heart sprinkles

24 black round sprinkles

Prep and Baking

1. Line a baking sheet with parchment paper. Set aside.

2. Make the cupcake batter per the recipe instructions. Line a 12-cup cupcake pan with cupcake liners and then fill the liners three-quarters full with the batter. Bake as instructed and allow to cool completely before decorating.

3. Make a batch of Basic Buttercream per the recipe instructions. Divide the buttercream into two equal-size portions. Color one portion yellow and transfer it to a piping bag fitted with piping tip 809. Color the second portion orange and transfer it to a piping bag fitted with piping tip 233. Secure the bags with clips.

Decorating

1. Use the yellow buttercream to pipe a dollop on top of each cupcake, leaving a ½-inch (1.25cm) gap around the edge. Hold the piping bag upright just above the center of the cupcake. Squeeze the bag until you have the desired amount of buttercream and then lift and pull away. *(see Photo 1)*

1

2

3

2. Press the cupcakes down onto the prepared baking sheet, leaving a ¼-inch (0.5cm) gap around the edge for the mane. (See "Using the Flip-and-Freeze Method" on page 18.) Transfer the baking sheet to the freezer for 15 to 20 minutes to allow the buttercream to set. Remove the baking sheet from the freezer and peel the cupcakes from the parchment paper. *(see Photo 2)*

3. Use the orange buttercream to pipe the fur around the edge of the cupcake. Hold the piping bag at an angle with the tip touching the cupcake. Squeeze out some buttercream and then pull away, releasing the pressure when you have the desired length of fur. Pipe a layer all the way around the face and then add a second layer. *(See Photo 3)*

4. To shape the face, add some fur to the top of the yellow buttercream. Start in the center and pipe an M shape. Fill in the gaps as needed. Add two yellow M&M's minis to the top of the face for the lion's ears. *(see Photo 4)*

5. To make the cheeks, roll out a piece of white fondant to ⅛ inch (3mm) thick. Use the large end of a small piping tip to cut out 24 circles. Use a toothpick to add small dots to the cheeks. Use tweezers to add two cheeks to each lion. *(see Photo 5)*

6. Use tweezers to add a heart sprinkle for the nose and two black round sprinkles for the eyes. *(see Photo 6)*

4

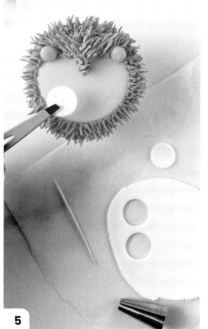
5

6

Sleepy Sloths

No hurry, be happy! If you're looking for a cute cupcake idea for a birthday, baby shower, or just a day hanging with your friends, these sleepy sloths are sure to bring some smiles. They look cute, taste great, and are so much fun to make.

Prep time

40 minutes

Baking time

20 minutes

Decorating time

40 minutes

Makes

12 cupcakes

EQUIPMENT

12-cup cupcake pan

12 cupcake liners

3 piping bags

1 large round piping tip (809)

1 small round piping tip (10)

1 small grass piping tip (233)

Baking sheet

Parchment paper

Tweezers

INGREDIENTS

12 Vanilla Cupcakes (p. 24)

1 batch Basic Buttercream (p. 33)

Brown food coloring

24 large black round sprinkles

24 black long sprinkles

Prep and Baking

1. Line a baking sheet with parchment paper. Set aside.

2. Make the cupcake batter per the recipe instructions. Line a 12-cup cupcake pan with cupcake liners and then fill the liners three-quarters full with the batter. Bake as instructed and allow to cool completely before decorating.

3. Make a batch of Basic Buttercream per the recipe instructions. Divide the buttercream into two equal-size portions. Color one portion pale brown and transfer it to a piping bag fitted with piping tip 809. Color the second portion a darker brown and transfer one-third of the buttercream to a piping bag fitted with piping tip 10 and then transfer the remaining buttercream to a piping bag fitted with piping tip 233. Secure the bags with clips.

Decorating

1. Use the pale brown buttercream to pipe a dollop on top of each cupcake, leaving a ½-inch (1.25cm) gap around the edge. Hold the piping bag upright and just above the center of the cupcake. Squeeze the bag until you have the correct amount of buttercream, then lift and pull away. *(see Photo 1)*

4   5   6

2. Press the cupcakes down onto the prepared baking sheet, leaving a ¼-inch (0.5cm) gap around the edge for the fur. (See "Using the Flip-and-Freeze Method" on page 18.) Transfer the baking sheet to the freezer for 15 to 20 minutes to allow the buttercream to set. Remove the baking sheet from the freezer and peel the cupcakes from the parchment paper.

3. Use the darker brown buttercream and piping tip 10 to add two lines on the sloth's face. Start at one side in the center of the face. Hold the piping bag upright and squeeze out a dot of buttercream. Continue squeezing a curved line, finishing at the edge of the face. Repeat this step on the opposite side. *(see Photo 2)*

4. Use the darker brown buttercream and piping tip 233 to pipe the fur around the edge of the cupcake. Hold the piping bag at an angle with the tip touching the cupcake. Squeeze out some buttercream and then pull away, releasing the pressure when you have the desired length of fur. Pipe a layer all the way around the face and then add a second layer. *(see Photo 3)*

5. To shape the face, add a line of fur across the top of the face. *(see Photo 4)*

6. From the center of the hairline, pipe longer fur that finishes over to the right-hand side. *(see Photo 5)*

7. Use tweezers to add two black round sprinkles for the eyes for 6 of the sloths; add long black sprinkles for the eyes on the remaining 6 sloths. Add a black round sprinkle for each nose and a long black sprinkle for the mouth. *(see Photo 6)*

Bunnies

It's so easy to use foil balls to turn cupcakes into cute bunnies! These adorable cupcakes will be the sweetest addition to a baby shower or birthday party, or just as a fun Easter treat. To make them extra fluffy, use piping tip 233 to pipe buttercream fur in place of the coconut. Cuteness overload!

Prep time
40 minutes

Baking time
20 minutes

Decorating time
30 minutes

Makes
12 cupcakes

EQUIPMENT

12-cup cupcake pan

12 foil cupcake liners

1 piping bag

1 large round piping tip (2A)

36 foil balls

Tweezers

INGREDIENTS

12 Carrot Cupcakes (p. 28)

1 batch Bright White Buttercream (p. 33)

100g (3.5oz) desiccated coconut

24 black round sprinkles

36 pink heart-shaped sprinkles

Prep and Baking

1. Make the cupcake batter per the recipe instructions. Line a 12-cup cupcake pan with foil cupcake liners and then fill the liners half full with the batter. Insert a foil ball into both sides of the liner, just above halfway, and add another foil ball in the middle at the top of the liner. (They should look like bunny ears.) Pinch the edges of the foil liners to help keep the shape during baking. Bake as instructed and allow to cool completely before decorating. *(see Photo 1)*

2. Make a batch of Bright White Buttercream per the recipe instructions. Transfer the buttercream to a piping bag fitted with tip 2A. Secure the bag with a clip.

Decorating

1. Use the white buttercream to pipe the shape of the bunny face. Pipe an oval-shaped swirl for the face, starting just below the ears and piping around the edges of the cupcake, finishing in the middle. Leave a ¼-inch (0.5cm) gap around the edges as the buttercream will spread a little when it is pushed into the coconut. *(see Photo 2)*

1

2

3

2. Pipe the ears by holding the piping bag at an angle with the tip touching the top side of the buttercream face. Squeeze and slowly pull upward, following the shape of the cupcake, then releasing the pressure and pulling away at the top of the cupcake. Repeat this step for the second ear, trying to make them as identical as possible. *(see Photo 3)*

3. Pour the desiccated coconut into a bowl and gently press the buttercream bunny into it. (Be careful not to push too hard or you'll lose the shape of the bunny.) To coat the sides, hold the cupcake over the bowl and use a spoon to pour the coconut over them. Once the buttercream is coated in coconut, you can gently press the sides to reshape, if needed. *(see Photo 4)*

4. Use tweezers to add two round black sprinkles for the eyes. Push them into the buttercream slightly to secure them into place. *(see Photo 5)*

5. Add a small amount of buttercream to the back of the sprinkle hearts before attaching them to the cupcake. Use tweezers to attach one for the nose and then two upside down for the pink parts of the ears. *(see Photo 6)*

4

5

6

Hip Hop Hooray! (Frogs)

Hip hop hooray! It's a froggy kind of day! Don't wait for Leap Day to make these hoppy little fellas. Jump into the kitchen and get started right away! You can swap the mini cupcake for a love heart for an engagement bash or Valentine's Day. Whatever the occasion, these toad-ally awesome treats will steal the show!

Prep time

40 minutes

Baking time

20 minutes

Decorating time

40 minutes

Makes

12 cupcakes

EQUIPMENT

12-cup cupcake pan

12 cupcake liners

5 piping bags

1 small open star piping tip (18)

1 jumbo round piping tip (809)

1 large round piping tip (2A)

1 small round piping tip (7)

Baking sheet

Parchment paper

Tweezers

INGREDIENTS

12 Chocolate Chip Cupcakes (p. 24)

1 batch Basic Buttercream (p. 33)

Food coloring (orange, green)

24 large candy eyes

6 Reese's Minis, each cut in half

24 pink round sprinkles

20g (0.75oz) black candy melts

Prep and Baking

1. Line a baking sheet with parchment paper. Set aside.

2. Make the cupcake batter per the recipe instructions. Line a 12-cup cupcake pan with cupcake liners and then fill the liners three-quarters full with the batter. Bake as instructed and allow to cool completely before decorating.

1

3. Make a batch of Basic Buttercream per the recipe instructions. Scoop out ½ cup and color it orange. Transfer it to a piping bag fitted with piping tip 18. Color the remaining buttercream pale green. Transfer a third of it to a piping bag fitted with piping tip 809. Transfer another third to a piping bag fitted with piping tip 2A. Transfer the remaining third to a piping bag fitted with piping tip 7. Secure the bags with clips.

Decorating

2

1. Pipe a dollop of the pale green buttercream on top of each cupcake, leaving a ¼-inch (0.5cm) gap around the edges. Hold the piping bag upright and just above the center of the cupcake. Squeeze the bag until you have the desired amount of buttercream, then lift and pull away. *(see Photo 1)*

3

2. Press the cupcakes down onto the prepared baking sheet. (See "Using the Flip-and-Freeze Method" on page 18.) Transfer the baking sheet to the freezer for 15 to 20 minutes to allow the buttercream to set. Remove the baking sheet from the freezer and peel the cupcakes from the parchment paper. *(see Photo 2)*

4

3. Use the green buttercream and piping tip 2A to pipe two large dots for the eyes to sit on. Hold the piping bag at the top left-hand side of the frog and then squeeze out a dot of buttercream. Release the pressure and pull away when you have the desired size. (Remember that the dot will spread when the candy eye is pressed onto it.) Do the same on the opposite side and then press the two large candy eyes into the buttercream. *(see Photo 3)*

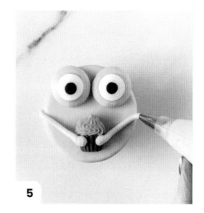

5

4. Place half of a Reese's Mini on the frog's belly. Use the orange buttercream and piping tip 18 to turn the Reese's Mini into a mini cupcake. Hold the piping bag at an angle with the tip just above one end of the Reese's Mini. Pipe a line back and forth, getting smaller each time, then pull away at the top. *(see Photo 4)*

5. Use the green buttercream and piping tip 7 to pipe the arms and legs. Hold the piping bag upright and just above the Reese's Mini. Squeeze a dot of buttercream, then continue squeezing a line going out and over to the side of the frog. Repeat this step for the other arm. *(see Photo 5)*

6

6. Pipe curved lines below each arm for the legs. Add three dots of buttercream for each foot. *(see Photo 6)*

7. Use tweezers to add two pink round sprinkles for the cheeks. *(see Photo 7)*

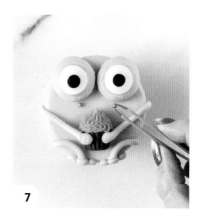

7

8. Heat the black candy melts in a microwave-safe bowl and transfer to a piping bag. (See "Working with Candy Melts" on page 21.) Cut a small hole in the end of the bag and pipe a smile. *(see Photo 8)*

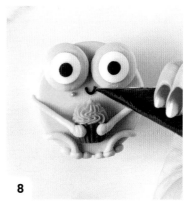

8

Pigs in the Mud

It's a pig party and you're invited! These pigs in the mud cupcakes are guaranteed to get some giggles at your next celebration. Served on a plate of crushed Oreo mud, what is not to love? Enjoy them for a farmyard-themed party, a baby shower, or just for pigging out with some friends.

Prep time
40 minutes

Baking time
20 minutes

Decorating time
30 minutes

Makes
12 cupcakes

EQUIPMENT

12-cup cupcake pan

12 pink foil cupcake liners

2 piping bags

1 large round piping tip (1A)

1 small round piping tip (7)

6 foil balls

Rolling pin

Tweezers

INGREDIENTS

12 Chocolate Cupcakes (p. 25)

1 batch Basic Buttercream (p. 33)

Pink food coloring

Pink sanding sugar

24 black round sprinkles

50g (1.75oz) pink fondant

10 Oreo cookies, cream centers removed and discarded

Prep and Baking

1. Make the cupcake batter per the recipe instructions. Line a 12-cup cupcake pan with cupcake liners. Fill 6 cupcake cups three-quarters full with batter.

2. Fill the remaining 6 cupcake cups half full with batter. Insert a foil ball at the bottom of the cupcake liners to create the shape of the pigs' bottoms. Bake as instructed and allow to cool completely before decorating. *(see Photo 1)*

1

3. Make a batch of Basic Buttercream per the instructions and color it pink. Add ¼ cup to a piping bag fitted with piping tip 7. Add the remaining buttercream to a piping bag fitted with piping tip 1A. Secure the bags with clips.

Decorating

1. To make the pigs' bottoms, use the pink buttercream and piping tip 1A and start at the bottom left corner. Hold the bag upright, squeeze out a large dot, then pull the buttercream up and in, releasing the pressure at the top of the cupcake. Repeat the process in the opposite direction. (The buttercream should resemble an upside-down heart shape.) *(see Photo 2)*

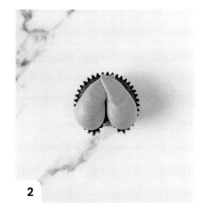

2

2. Pour the pink sanding sugar into a small bowl and gently press the buttercream into the sugar. (If the line down the center of the cupcake isn't straight, make an indent by pressing a cocktail stick or toothpick lengthwise into the buttercream.) Set aside. *(see Photo 3)*

3

3. To make the pigs' faces, use the pink buttercream and piping tip 1A to pipe a dollop of buttercream in the center of each cupcake, leaving a ¼-inch (0.5cm) gap around the edges. Hold the bag upright with the tip touching the cupcake and then squeeze while lifting the bag and pulling away. *(see Photo 4)*

4

4. Press the cupcakes into the pink sanding sugar and swirl the cupcake until the buttercream has spread to the edges and the sugar is covering the top evenly. *(see Photo 5)*

5. Roll out the pink fondant to around ¹⁄₁₀ inch (3mm) thickness. Use the end of a large piping tip to cut out 18 circles (6 snouts and 12 ears). *(see Photo 6)*

6. For the 6 snouts, add two black round sprinkles for nostrils. For the ears, pinch two opposite ends of each circle together to make an eye shape. Let them sit for 15 minutes to firm up slightly, then cut the point off one end of each ear. Attach the snouts and ears with a small amount of buttercream. *(see Photo 7)*

7. Use tweezers to add two black round sprinkles for the eyes. *(see Photo 8)*

8. Use the pink buttercream and piping tip 7 to add tails to the pigs' bottoms. Hold the piping bag upright above the cupcake, squeeze out a small dot, and move the tip in a circle around the dot, moving up in a spiral until you reach the desired height. Stop squeezing before pulling the tip away. *(see Photo 9)*

9. For the mud, add the Oreo cookies to a food processor and process into crumbs. (Alternatively, place the cookies in a plastic ziplock bag and crush them with a rolling pin.) Pour the crushed Oreos out onto a large serving plate and arrange the cupcakes on top. *(see Photo 10)*

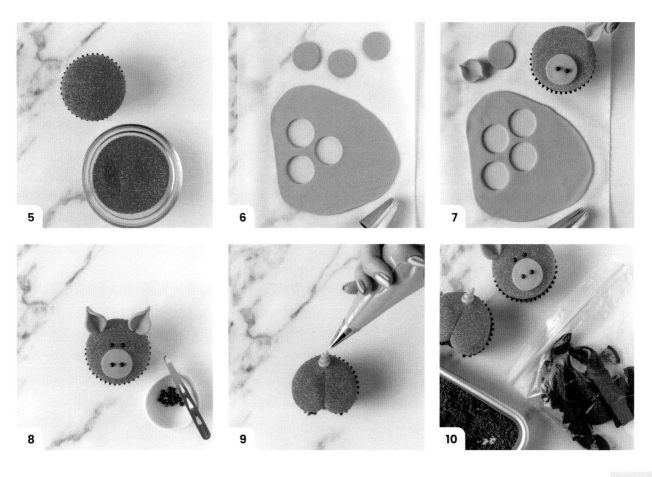

5   6   7

8   9   10

Prep time
1 hour

Baking time
20 minutes

Decorating time
1 hour

Makes
12 cupcakes

Penguins

If you're looking for a fun and festive baking project this winter, look no further than these cute little penguin cupcakes. Made with yummy chocolate cupcakes and decorated with vanilla and black cocoa buttercreams, they taste as good as they look. They're perfect for a winter party, a Christmas celebration, or even just an activity for a rainy day.

EQUIPMENT

12-cup cupcake pan

12 foil cupcake liners

2 piping bags

1 large round piping tips (2A)

1 small round piping tip (12)

Baking sheet

Parchment paper

24 foil balls

Tweezers

INGREDIENTS

12 Chocolate Cupcakes (p. 25)

1 batch Basic Buttercream (p. 33)

40g (1.5oz) black or dark cocoa

2 tbsp heavy cream

¼ tsp black food coloring gel

100g (3.5oz) desiccated coconut

24 black sprinkles

36 orange candies (M&M's or Reese's Pieces)

Prep and Baking

1. Line a baking sheet with parchment paper. Set aside.

2. Make the cupcake batter per the recipe instructions. Line a 12-cup cupcake pan with foil liners and then fill the liners half-full with the batter. Insert a foil ball into both sides of the liner to create the penguin shape, making the top part slightly smaller than the bottom. Pinch the corners of the liners to keep the shape while the cupcakes are baking. Bake as instructed and allow to cool completely before decorating. *(see Photo 1)*

3. Make a batch of Basic Buttercream per the recipe instructions. Transfer one-third of the buttercream to a piping bag fitted with piping tip 12. Add the black or dark cocoa, heavy cream, and the black food coloring gel to the remaining buttercream. Mix until smooth. Transfer to a piping bag fitted with piping tip 2A. Seal the bags with clips.

Decorating

1. Pipe a larger circle of chocolate buttercream at the bottom of the cupcake for the body, then pipe a smaller circle of chocolate buttercream in the center of the top part of the cupcake for the head, leaving ¼-inch (0.5cm) gaps around both circles as the buttercream will spread when the cupcakes are pressed down. *(see Photo 2)*

2. Gently press the cupcakes down onto the prepared baking sheet, and transfer the baking sheet to the freezer for 15 to 20 minutes. (See "Using the Flip-and-Freeze Method" on page 18.) Remove the cupcakes from the freezer and peel them from the parchment paper.

3. Using the white buttercream, pipe two lines down and then a round swirl underneath. (This will look just like a bunny.) Very carefully press the cupcakes into the desiccated coconut until the white buttercream is covered. *(see Photo 3)*

4. Use tweezers to add black sprinkles for the eyes and orange candies for the beaks and feet. *(see Photo 4)*

Pupcakes

These cupcakes are the perfect treat for your next pup party! Make these super-cute pupcakes for a birthday party or for a dog lover, or add Santa hats to create Christmas pugs. The Oreo buttercream wrinkles and black cocoa cheeks make these as delicious as they are adorable. They're nearly too sweet to eat!

Prep time
40 minutes

Baking time
20 minutes

Decorating time
1 hour

Makes
12 cupcakes

EQUIPMENT

12-cup cupcake pan

12 cupcake liners

2 piping bags

1 large round piping tip (1A)

1 small round piping tip (7)

Cling film

Small serrated knife

Tweezers

INGREDIENTS

12 Flavored Cupcakes (p. 24)

1 batch Basic Buttercream (p. 33)

25g (1oz) black cocoa powder

3 tbsp heavy cream, divided

¼ tsp black food coloring gel

5 Oreo cookies, crushed into crumbs

2 drops brown food coloring

36 black round sugar pearls

12 pink heart-shaped sprinkles

12 mini Oreo cookies, separated and cream centers removed

1   2   3

Prep and Baking

1. Make the cupcake batter per the recipe instructions. Line a 12-cup cupcake pan with cupcake liners and then fill the liners two-thirds full with the batter. Bake as instructed and allow to cool completely before decorating.

2. Make a batch of Basic Buttercream per the recipe instructions. Transfer half the buttercream to a bowl, cover it with cling film, and set it aside. Add the remaining buttercream, the black cocoa powder, half of the heavy cream, and the black food gel coloring to the bowl of a stand mixer. Mix on low until you have a smooth consistency. Transfer the buttercream to a piping bag fitted with piping tip 1A. Secure the bag with a clip.

3. Add the crushed Oreos, remaining heavy cream, and brown food coloring to the bowl with the reserved buttercream. Mix until combined. Transfer to a piping bag fitted with piping tip 7. Secure the bag with a clip.

4

5

Decorating

1. Use the black buttercream to add the cheeks. Hold the piping bag upright and just above the bottom left-hand side of the cupcake. Squeeze out a large dot of buttercream and then move the bag up toward the center of the cupcake. Release the pressure and pull away to the right. Repeat this step for the opposite cheek. Use tweezers to add a black round sugar pearl for the nose. *(see Photo 1)*

2. Use the Oreo buttercream to add the wrinkles. Hold the bag to the left-hand side of the cupcake. Starting just above the cheek, pipe a line all the way across the top of the black buttercream. Pipe two dots above the line for the eyes. *(see Photo 2)*

3. Push a black round sugar pearl onto each buttercream dot. Continue piping lines around the eyes and the rest of the face. *(see Photo 3)*

4. Use a small serrated knife to gently saw each mini Oreo half into a triangle. Add a small amount of buttercream to the back of each triangle, and attach them to the cupcakes to create the ears. *(see Photo 4)*

5. Use tweezers to add a heart-shaped sprinkle to the middle of the buttercream cheeks for the tongue. *(see Photo 5)*

Acknowledgments

My wonderful husband: Donal

Thank you for being you, so positive and encouraging. For believing in me, especially when I don't, and for the countless times you have talked me out of my self-doubt. You're always there when I need you. Without you, none of this would have been possible. Thank you for everything you do for me and the boys; we are so lucky to have you.

My gorgeous children: Conor, Liam, and Ronan

Thank you for blessing every day with fun, laughter, and craziness. Our home is so loud and chaotic, and I wouldn't have it any other way. From taste testing to choosing the most outrageous birthday cakes, you boys have played such a huge part in my cake-decorating journey. Thank you for understanding that I have been busy and for being good for Daddy. I am so proud of you all. Love you.

Mum and Dad

For traveling to the other side of the world to visit me and to help me with the boys while I'm busy playing with cupcakes. For teaching me that hard work pays off and always supporting me and my creative impulses. Dad, thank you for encouraging me to follow my dreams, for letting me know that you are proud of me, and always making me laugh out loud. Mum, I would be lost without you, my best friend. Thank you for always being on the end of the phone when I need you; somehow, talking to you makes everything better. I love you and miss you so much.

Harriet

I am so lucky that I got to do this with you. You are amazing at what you do. Thank you for the most beautiful photographs, for your kindness, and for holding my hand through an intense three weeks. We had so much fun together. We did it.

Brook

I couldn't have asked for a better writing partner. From the very first email, you have been so kind and wonderful. You have been a joy to work with and a pleasure to get to know. Thank you for guiding me, for being patient with me, and for helping me become an author. I still can't believe it. I am so grateful to you.

Bill

For being so good at what you do. I don't know how you did it; it's like you read my mind. The vision that you had for the design of this book is perfect. I absolutely love it. Thank you.

The DK team

Thank you for believing in me. You saw my passion and helped me bring a dream to life. I feel very lucky that I got to do this with such an amazing team. Thank you so much for your continued support.

Friends and family, near and far

There are so many of you to thank, I could be here all day. Thank you for supporting me, encouraging me, and showing an interest in what I do. I could never have dreamed I would be here when I made my first cake 12 years ago. I appreciate you all.

My followers and cake community

Without you, none of this would be possible. I am so grateful to each and every one of you. Thank you for the constant love and support, encouragement, and kindness. I hope this book brings you happiness and inspires you to push your creative boundaries.

Index

allspice, Chai Latte Cupcakes, 31
animals, cupcakes based on
    Bunnies, 217–19
    Hip Hop Hooray!, 221–23
    Kings of the Jungle, 209–11
    Penguins, 228–29
    Pigs in the Mud, 225–27
    Pupcakes, 231–33
    Sleepy Sloths, 213–15
    Turtle-y Awesome, 205–7
apple cider vinegar, Red Velvet
    Cupcakes, 26
avocados. See Happy Avocados

baby shower cupcakes. See It's a
    Baby!
baking trays, 12
Basic Buttercream, 33
    BBQ Grills, 141–43
    Bird Nests, 59–61
    Cactuses, 161–63
    Campfires, 137–39
    Cheeseburgers, 181–83
    Easter Baskets, 63–65
    Flower Pots, 157–59
    Graduation Caps, 122–23
    Happy Birthday!, 111–13
    Hot Dogs, 178–79
    It's a Baby!, 125–29
    Kings of the Jungle, 209–11
    Love Monsters, 43–45
    Melting Ice Creams, 175–77
    Mister Brain, 66–67
    Mother's Day Flower Power,
        131–33
    Penguins, 228–29
    Pigs in the Mud, 225–27
    Pineapples, 199–201
    Pumpkin Patch, 169–71
    Pupcakes, 231–33
    Shamrocks, 47–49
    Shaped Christmas Trees, 89–91
    Sleepy Sloths, 213–15
    Snow-Covered Christmas
        Trees, 93–95
    Spaghetti and Meatballs,
        184–85

Toadstools, 145–47
    Turtle-y Awesome, 205–7
BBQ Grills, 141–43
Beach Vibes, 153–55
Bird Nests, 59–61
birthday cupcakes
    Birthday Magic!, 115–17
    Happy Birthday!, 111–13
Birthday Magic!, 115–17
Black Buttercream, 37
    Pots of Gold, 51–53
black cocoa powder, 14. See also
    cocoa powder
bridal showers. See High Heels
Bright White Buttercream, 33
    Bunnies, 217–19
    Frosty and Friends, 97–99
    Ghosts, 77–79
    High Heels, 119–21
    Santas, 101–3
    Spooky Skulls, 69–71
    Sushi Train, 191–93
    Wedding Day, 107–9
Bunnies, 217–19
Bunny Butts, 54–55. See also
    Easter Baskets; Easter Chicks
buttercream
    coloring, 17
    flip-and-freeze method, 21
    piping and, 19
    recipes, 24–37
Buttercream & Cupcake Recipes
    Basic Buttercream, 33
    Black Buttercream, 37
    Carrot Cupcakes, 28
    Chai Latte Cupcakes, 31
    Chocolate Buttercream, 34
    Chocolate Cupcakes, 25
    Cookie Dough Cupcakes, 32
    Cream Cheese
        Buttercream, 36
    Flavored Cupcakes, 24
    Hybrid Buttercream, 36
    Lemon Cupcakes, 29
    Oreo Buttercream, 34
    Peanut Butter and Jelly
        Cupcakes, 27
    Rainbow Cupcakes, 30
    Red Velvet Cupcakes, 26
    Swiss Meringue
        Buttercream, 35
    Vanilla Cupcakes, 24
Butterflies, 149–51

Cactuses, 161–63
Campfires, 137–39
candy eyes
    Hip Hop Hooray!, 221–23
    Love Monsters, 43–45
    Mister Brain, 66–67
    Turkeys, 81–83
candy melts, 14, 21
    BBQ Grills, 141–43
    Bunny Butts, 54–55
    Easter Baskets, 63–65
    Flower Pots, 157–59
    Ghosts, 77–79
    Happy Avocados, 195–97
    High Heels, 119–21
    Hip Hop Hooray!, 221–23
    It's a Baby!, 125–29
    Melting Ice Creams, 175–77
    Mother's Day Flower Power,
        131–33
    Pineapples, 199–201
    Shamrocks, 47–49
    Spaghetti and
        Meatballs,184–85
    Spooky Skulls, 69–71
    Wedding Day, 107–9
    Witches' Hats, 74–75
candy straws, Sushi Train, 191–93
cardamom, Chai Latte
    Cupcakes, 31
Carrot Cupcakes, 28
    Bird Nests, 59–61
    Bunnies, 217–19
    Bunny Butts, 54–55
carrots, Carrot Cupcakes, 28
caster sugar, 14
Chai Latte Cupcakes, 31
    Kings of the Jungle, 209–11
    Oh My, Pumpkin Pies!, 85–87
    Pumpkin Patch, 169–71
    Santas, 101–3
    Witches' Hats, 73–75
Chai Spice Mix, Chai Latte
    Cupcakes, 31
Cheeseburgers, 181–83
Chocolate Buttercream, 34
    Birthday Magic!, 115–17
    Pine Cones, 165–67
Chocolate Chip Cupcakes, 24
    High Heels, 119–21
    Hip Hop Hooray!, 221–23

chocolate chips
    Chocolate Cupcakes, 25
    Cookie Dough Cupcakes, 32
Chocolate Cupcakes, 25
    Birthday Magic!, 115–17
    Easter Baskets, 63–65
    Frosty and Friends, 97–99
    Pigs in the Mud, 225–27
    Pine Cones, 165–67
    Pots of Gold, 51–53
    Shaped Christmas Trees,
        89–91
    Turkeys, 81–83
Christmas, cupcakes for
    Frosty and Friends, 97–99
    Santas, 101–3
    Shaped Christmas Trees,
        89–91
    Snow-Covered Christmas
        Trees, 93–95
cinnamon
    Carrot Cupcakes, 28
    Chai Latte Cupcakes, 31
cocktail umbrellas, Beach Vibes,
    153–55
cocoa powder, 14
    BBQ Grills, 141–43
    Bird Nests, 59–61
    Black Buttercream, 37
    Cheeseburgers, 181–83
    Chocolate Buttercream, 34
    Chocolate Cupcakes, 25
    Flower Pots, 157–59
    Mother's Day Flower Power,
        131–33
    Oreo Buttercream, 34
    Pupcakes, 231–33
    Red Velvet Cupcakes, 26
coconut
    Bunnies, 217–19
    Bunny Butts, 54–55
    Frosty and Friends, 97–99
    Penguins, 228–29
    Pine Cones, 165–67
    Snow-Covered Christmas
        Trees, 93–95
    Sushi Train, 191–93
confectioners' sugar, 14
Cookie Dough Cupcakes
    Melting Ice Creams, 175–77
    Snow-Covered Christmas
        Trees, 93–95
cookie dough scoop, 12

Cream Cheese Buttercream, 36
    Bunny Butts, 54–55
    Easter Chicks, 56–57
cupcakes
    animals, 203–33
    basic ingredients for, 14–15
    Buttercream & Cupcake
        Recipes, 23–37
    coloring buttercream, 21
    creating shaped cupcakes, 20
    essential equipment for
        making, 12–13
    flip-and-freeze method, 21
    food, 173–201
    holidays, 39–101
    seasonal cupcakes, 135–71
    for special occasions, 107–33
    working with candy melts, 21

D

daisies. *See* Mother's Day
    Flower Power
dark chocolate
    Birthday Magic!, 115–17
    Black Buttercream, 37
desiccated coconut, 14. *See
    also* coconut
digital scale, 12

E

Easter Baskets, 63–65
Easter Chicks, 56–57
eggs, 14

F

fall, cupcakes for
    Pumpkin Patch, 169–71
    Pine Cones, 165–67
Flavored Cupcakes, 24
    Beach Vibes, 153–55
    Pineapples, 199–201
    Pupcakes, 231–33
flavorings, 14
flour, 14
Flower Pots, 157–59
fondant, 14
    Bunny Butts, 54–55
    Kings of the Jungle, 209–11
    Pigs in the Mud, 225–27
    Shaped Christmas Trees,
        89–91

Snow-Covered Christmas
    Trees, 93–95
Sushi Train, 191–93
food coloring, 14–15
Happy Avocados, 195–97
    Penguins, 228–29
    Pigs in the Mud, 225–27
    Pineapples, 199–201
Pupcakes, 231–33
    Sleepy Sloths, 213–15
    Sushi Train, 191–93
    Turtle-y Awesome, 205–7
food, cupcakes based on
    Cheeseburgers, 181–83
    Fruit Pies, 187–89
    Happy Avocados, 195–97
    Hot Dogs, 178–79
    Melting Ice Creams, 175–77
    Pineapples, 199–201
    Spaghetti and Meatballs,
        184–85
    Sushi Train, 191–93
frogs. *See* Hip Hop Hooray!
Frosty and Friends, 97–99
Fruit Pies, 187–89
Funfetti Cupcakes, 24
    Mother's Day Flower Power,
        131–33
    Turtle-y Awesome, 205–7

G

gelatin powder, Turtle-y
    Awesome, 205–7
gender reveal cupcakes. *See* It's
    a Baby!
Ghosts, 77–79
ginger, Chai Latte Cupcakes, 31
Graduation Caps, 122–23
grill cupcakes. *See* BBQ Grills
gummy bears, BBQ Grills, 141–43

H

Haribo fruits, Sushi Train, 191–93
Halloween, cupcakes for
    Ghosts, 77–79
    Mister Brain, 66–67
    Oh My, Pumpkin Pies!, 85–87
    Spooky Skulls, 69–71
    Witches' Hats, 73–75
Happy Avocados, 195–97
Happy Birthday!, 111–13
Hershey's Whoppers, Spaghetti
    and Meatballs, 184–85

High Heels, 119–21
Hip Hop Hooray!, 221–23
holidays, cupcakes for
    Bird Nests, 59–61
    Bunny Butts, 54–55
    Easter Baskets, 63–65
    Easter Chicks, 56–57
    Frosty and Friends, 97–99
    Ghosts, 77–79
    Love Hearts, 40–41
    Love Monsters, 43–45
    Mister Brain, 66–67
    Oh My, Pumpkin Pies!, 85–87
    Pots of Gold, 51–53
    Santas, 101–3
    Shamrocks, 47–49
    Shaped Christmas Trees,
        89–91
    Snow-Covered Christmas
        Trees, 93–95
    Spooky Skulls, 69–71
    Turkeys, 81–83
    Witches' Hats, 73–75
Hot Dogs, 178–79
Hybrid Buttercream, 36
    Beach Vibes, 153–55
    Butterflies, 149–51
    Fruit Pies, 187–89
    Love Hearts, 40–41
    Oh My, Pumpkin Pies!, 85–87

I–K

It's a Baby!, 125–29

jelly beans, It's a Baby!, 125–29

Kings of the Jungle, 209–11
kitchen timer, 12

L

Lemon Cupcakes, 29
    Butterflies, 149–51
    Cactuses, 161–63
    Campfires, 137–39
    Easter Chicks, 56–57
    Toadstools, 145–47
    Wedding Day, 107–9
lemons, Lemon Cupcakes, 29
Life Savers, It's a Baby!, 125–29
lime gelation packets, Turtle-y
    Awesome, 205–7
Lindt truffles, Happy Avocados,

195–97
liners, 12
lions. See Kings of the Jungle
Love Hearts, 40–41
Love Monsters, 43–45

M

M&M's
    Birthday Magic!, 115–17
    Easter Chicks, 56–57
    Fruit Pies, 187–89
    Graduation Caps, 122–23
    Kings of the Jungle, 209–11
    Penguins, 228–29
    Santas, 101–3
    Turkeys, 81–83
marshmallows
    Bunny Butts, 54–55
    Campfires, 137–39
measuring spoon, 12
melts. See candy melts
Melting Ice Creams, 175–77
milk chocolate squares,
    Graduation Caps, 122–23
mini chocolate eggs, Easter
    Baskets, 63–65
mini ice cream cones, Melting Ice
    Creams, 175–77
mini pretzels, Shamrocks, 47–49
Mister Brain, 66–67
mixing bowls, 12
Mother's Day Flower Power, 131–33
multicolored swirl, piping, 22

N

Nestlé Chocapic chocolate cereal,
    Pine Cones, 165–67
nonpareils, Sushi Train, 191–93
Nutella Swirl Cupcakes, 24
    Spaghetti and Meatballs,
        184–85
Nutella, Happy Avocados, 195–97
nutmeg, Carrot Cupcakes, 28

O

Oh My, Pumpkin Pies!, 85–87
Oreo Buttercream, 34
Oreo cookies
    Campfires, 137–39
    Flower Pots, 157–59
    Love Monsters, 43–45
    Mother's Day Flower Power,
        131–33

    Oreo Buttercream, 34
    Pigs in the Mud, 225–27
    Pumpkin Patch, 169–71
    Pupcakes, 231–33
oven thermometer, 12

P

palette knives, 12
pans, 12
parchment paper, 12
Peanut Butter and Jelly
    Cupcakes, 27
    BBQ Grills, 141–43
peanut butter, Peanut Butter and
    Jelly Cupcakes, 27
Penguins, 228–29
Pepperidge Farm Milano cookies,
    High Heels, 119–21
Pigs in the Mud, 225–27
Pine Cones, 165–67
piping bags, 12–13, 15–16, 19
Pocky Sticks
    BBQ Grills, 141–43
    Birthday Magic!, 115–17
    Cactuses, 161–63
    Flower Pots, 157–59
    Love Monsters, 43–45
    Pineapples, 199–201
    Pumpkin Patch, 169–71
    Snow-Covered Christmas
        Trees, 93–95
Pots of Gold, 51–53
pretzel sticks
    Campfires, 137–39
    Shamrocks, 47–49
Pumpkin Patch, 169–71
Pupcakes, 231–33

R

rainbow belt candies, Pots of Gold,
    51–53
Rainbow Cupcakes, 30
    Happy Birthday!, 111–13
    Hot Dogs, 178–79
    Love Monsters, 43–45
    Mister Brain, 66–67
    Shamrocks, 47–49
rainbow sprinkles
    Melting Ice Creams, 175–77
    Shamrocks, 47–49
Red Velvet Cupcakes, 26
    Graduation Caps, 122–23

Love Hearts, 40–41
Spooky Skulls, 69–71
Reese's Miniature Cups
Ghosts, 77–79
Graduation Caps, 122–23
Happy Birthday!, 111–13
Hip Hop Hooray!, 221–23
Shaped Christmas Trees, 89–91
Turkeys, 81–83
Reese's Pieces
Easter Chicks, 56–57
Penguins, 228–29
rolled wafer cookies, High Heels, 119–21
rubber spatulas, 13

S

sanding sugar, 15
Santas, 101–3
seasonal cupcakes
BBQ Grills, 141–43
Beach Vibes, 153–55
Butterflies, 149–51
Cactuses, 161–63
Campfires, 137–39
Flower Pots, 157–59
Pine Cones, 165–67
Pumpkin Patch, 169–71
Toadstools, 145–47
serrated knife, 12
Shamrocks, 47–49
Shaped Christmas Trees, 89–91
shaped cupcakes, creating, 20
shortbread cookies
Beach Vibes, 153–55
Cactuses, 161–63
Turtle-y Awesome, 205–7
Sleepy Sloths, 213–15
sloths. See Sleepy Sloths
Snow-Covered Christmas Trees, 93–95
snowmen. See Frosty and Friends
Spaghetti and Meatballs, 184–85
special occasions, cupcakes for
Birthday Magic!, 115–17
Graduation Caps, 122–23
Happy Birthday!, 111–13
High Heels, 119–21
It's a Baby!, 125–29
Mother's Day Flower Power, 131–33

Wedding Day, 107–9
Spooky Skulls, 69–71
spring, cupcakes for
Bird Nests, 59–61
Butterflies, 149–51
Flower Pots, 157–59
Toadstools, 145–47
sprinkles and decorations, 15
Butterflies, 149–51
Easter Chicks, 56–57
Frosty and Friends, 97–99
Happy Avocados, 195–97
Hip Hop Hooray!, 221–23
It's a Baby!, 125–29
Kings of the Jungle, 209–11
Pigs in the Mud, 225–27
Santas, 101–3
Sleepy Sloths, 213–15
Turtle-y Awesome, 205–7
St. Patrick's Day, cupcakes for
Pots of Gold, 51–53
Shamrocks, 47–49
stand mier, 13
strawberry dessert sauce
Mister Brain, 66–67
Spooky Skulls, 69–71
Strawberry Jam Cupcakes, 24
Flower Pots, 157–59
strawberry jam, Peanut Butter and Jelly Cupcakes, 27
strawberry laces, Graduation Caps, 122–23
sugar cones, Witches' Hats, 73–75
sugar pearls
High Heels, 119–21
Pots of Gold, 51–53
Pupcakes, 231–33
Snow-Covered Christmas Trees, 93–95
Wedding Day, 107–9
summer, cupcakes for
BBQ Grills, 141–43
Beach Vibes, 153–55
Campfires, 137–39
Cactuses, 161–63
sunflowers. See Mother's Day Flower Power
Sushi Train, 191–93
Swedish Fish, Sushi Train, 191–93
Swiss Meringue Buttercream, 35
Turkeys, 81–83
Witches' Hats, 73–75

T

Teddy Grahams, Beach Vibes, 153–55
Thanksgiving, cupcakes for. See Turkeys
Toadstools, 145–47
toothpicks, 13
Turkeys, 81–83
Turtle-y Awesome, 205–7
tweezers, 13

U–V

unsalted butter, 15

Valentine's Day, cupcakes for. See Love Hearts; Love Monsters
Vanilla Cupcakes, 24
Cheeseburgers, 181–83
Ghosts, 77–79
Happy Avocados, 195–97
It's a Baby!, 125–29
Sleepy Sloths, 213–15
Sushi Train, 191–93
vanilla extract, 15
Black Buttercream, 37
Carrot Cupcakes, 28
Chai Latte Cupcakes, 31
Cookie Dough Cupcakes, 32
Flavored Cupcakes, 24
Hybrid Buttercream, 36
Rainbow Cupcakes, 30
Red Velvet Cupcakes, 26
Swiss Meringue Buttercream, 35
Vanilla Cupcakes, 25

W–Z

walnuts, Carrot Cupcakes, 28
Wedding Day, 107–9
whisk, 13
winter, cupcakes for
Frosty and Friends, 97–99
Santas, 101–3
Shaped Christmas Trees, 89–91
Snow-Covered Christmas Trees, 93–95
Witches' Hats, 73–75

About the Author

Rachel Lindsay is the creative force behind Caked by Rach on TikTok, Instagram, and YouTube, where she shares her clever cupcake creations with over 3 million fans worldwide. Rachel discovered her love for baking and decorating cakes in 2012 when she made her son's christening cake. She enjoyed it so much that she started creating cakes for just about any occasion you can think of. She started with fondant-covered cakes with handmade figures on top but would spend hours baking and decorating cakes. As her family grew, life got busy and there was no time for cake decorating. But in 2020, she felt she was missing something creative and it was then that she discovered her love for creating cupcakes. Her first attempts at using piping tips and buttercreams were disasters, but she persisted and practiced, and that was the start of Caked by Rach.

Rachel was born and raised in Lancashire, UK, but currently resides in Perth, Western Australia, with her husband and three children. You can find Rachel online at cakedbyrach.com.